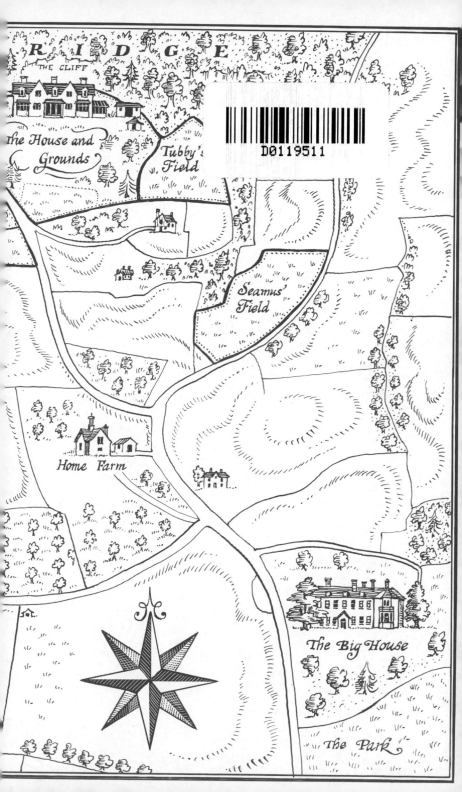

# A BUCKET OF NUTS
# AND A HERRING NET

# A Bucket of Nuts
# and a Herring Net

## The Birth
## of a Spare-time Farm

JOHN JACKSON

*Illustrated by Val Biro*

COLLINS and HARVILL PRESS
London, 1979

© 1979 John Jackson
ISBN 0 00 262045 6

Set in Linotype Pilgrim

Made and printed in Great Britain by
William Collins Sons & Co Ltd, Glasgow
for Collins, St James's Place and
Harvill Press, 30A Pavilion Road, London SW1

*To Fleur*
*and the other friends*
*who have lived with us*

# Contents

## PROLOGUE

# The Ridge

We live in the country, well inside the commuter belt. The reason for this paradox is the ridge. The ridge forms the high northern edge of a thin tongue of woods and farmland, curling across the countryside from east to west, less than twenty-five miles from the heart of London, as the crow flies.

Little villages and farmsteads, dependent on the belt of land protected by the ridge from the cold north winds, have snuggled against its warm southern footings from the time of the Domesday Book and before. Some of them have names which pay tribute to the ridge in pure Saxon tongue. The top of the ridge has always carried a belt of thick woodland giving shelter to wild things and a source of fuel and building material to the households below.

This state of affairs was settled so long ago that, with no help from modern planners, the sprawl of London's satellites falters and peters out to the north of the ridge as it meets the belt of woodland. It slowly resumes its steady march after it has passed the farmland to the south. From time to time new settlers have tackled the steep southern slopes of the ridge. But there the clays and springs shift about, cracking foundations, breaking water mains and forcing electricity supplies to be run above ground. The only major road built to cross the ridge in recent times had to be re-routed when half-completed. A finished section slid yards down the hillside one wet night. The local villagers smiled. The same fate had overtaken a newly built house nearby some thirty years before. The ridge resents intruders. The first people to harness the hostility of the ridge were the Victorian builders of the railway tunnel. The springs which continually flooded their workings were led away to become the foundation source of the local water company.

The ridge has tolerated the building of a few houses. Ours is one of them. A cart track running at right angles off a narrow minor road, which creeps cautiously down from the crest, ends at our house on the edge of woodland. The house is built mainly of ragstone dug from off the site. It sits long and low on a shelf of land formed by an ancient landslip from the edge of the ridge. Behind the house to the north is a long steep cliff, some sixty feet high, left by the slip. To the south our grounds plunge down and away in a series of terraces with a mean slope of about one in seven.

Although the landslip happened long ago, the shelf on which the house sits is slowly tipping down the hill. The shelf itself contains a layer of ragstone and greensand, but below this is clay. The winter rains rush through the sand and rock, saturate the clay beneath and trickle out as a series of springs all the year round. The wet clay beneath bulges and heaves, pressed down by the weight of the rock and sand above, quite changing the contours of the lower slopes of the hillside from year to year. As more of the clay bulges out, so the shelf above tips a little more down the hill. The oldest part of our house, the original two up and two down stone cottage set down on the ground with no foundations, has leaned down the hill some two inches in seven vertical feet over its 150 years. The rest of the house has been added at five different times and each of those additions is leaning at its own pace. The dramatic cracks which result are filled in by us each spring and autumn. It is always the same cracks which re-open. They have an insatiable appetite for mortar and fillers. Lying in bed on a still night you can hear the creaking and cracking as the leaning goes on. It does not worry us too much, but we are not very popular with the building societies.

We look out on an immense view over the Wealds of Kent and Sussex. We can always see the weather changes coming up from the south-west. While the woods to the east and the cliff to the north protect us from the cold winds, the south-westerly gales come roaring up the hill, over the fields and garden and fairly blast us. The woods and the cliff do not protect us from the snow. 'It may fall as snow on high ground' is a warning in the weather reports which we have to take seriously. Many times we have been living in our own private snow field while the village below us has been simply wet and green.

The village is important to us. We belong to it. Before we came to the house, we lived some five miles away in real commuter territory and did not belong to anything. It was all right for me for so long as I burned with the ambition to be a red-hot business executive and little more. 'Ten minutes' walk to the station' for my daily trip to London was very convenient. Home was mainly where I ate and slept during the week and gardened or watched television at the weekend. It was not so nice for the rest of the family. Ann, my wife, frankly loathed it. She had lived in a country village for much of her life and she missed being woven into the fabric of a community. Good friends scattered around in other roads leading to the station were no substitute.

Matters became worse when other people in our road started selling half their gardens off as building lots. The uncomfortable feeling that we were being hemmed in began to grow in us. The morning procession to the station became an urgent jostling flood. The trains were so crowded that the wear and tear of making the journey daily by car became the lesser of two evils. The turning point came when it was clear that the countryside tugged at our three children too. Mark, our son and the oldest, was forever pestering me for a day's fishing. Sue, the elder of the two girls, was dewy-eyed over ponies and practically lived as a grubby unpaid help at the nearest riding stable. Carol Jane, C-J for short, was too young to be left far out of sight anywhere, but the atmosphere of growing frustration at home set her teeth on edge and made her fractious.

Ann found the ridge and started a deliberate process of slow, subtle seduction. She took the children for picnics in its woodlands during the summer holidays. In the early autumn, the four of them went blackberrying. It was then they found the village. They also found a barn half-converted for habitation. By some quirk of the planning regulations, permission to finish the job was available on demand. It was a wildly impracticable proposition for anyone with our financial resources and I fought it off with ease.

Ann stumbled on the house, hidden away below the cliff, in the spring. It had been lived in for many years by very elderly people. The house had decayed with them. It found its way into the hands of an astute estate agent who had put it in reasonable order. The estate agent's wife was a French girl. She was used to towns and had difficulties with English. The isolation of the house added to her sense of loneliness and her husband decided to take his profit and sell. I suspect that those awesome cracks which keep reappearing in the walls and ceilings had something to do with it too. By sheer chance Ann heard of the situation before he put the house on the open market.

I was taken out to see it on a dry spring day. The sky was blue. Birds were singing. The sunlight picked out the greys and purples in the tops of the trees and the soft yellow of primroses pushing through the carpets of fallen leaves beneath. The cliff protected us from an icy north wind and the view was at its magnificent best. The whole atmosphere was inviting and the wildness of the garden with its scrub and woodland added to the feeling of adventure. Possible uses for the newly constructed paddock at the bottom of the garden were lost on none of us. I don't believe we heard a single word the owner or his wife said to us.

It was one of those now or never situations. We decided it had to be now. The family was over the moon with joy. I had an uneasy feeling that we had been rash. I was right. I spent a ghastly six months doing the bridging loan splits while we tried to sell the old house on a falling market. We moved in the December on a filthy wet day. Mark was ten, Sue was eight and C-J was four. Ann looked and behaved like a teenager. I was at least a hundred.

The village made us welcome. Newcomers were a rarity so we were submitted to a polite inquisitive scrutiny. This was done in the gentlest possible way as we were instructed on features of the village that were important for us to know. Some of the more obvious things we knew already. The village had no shops and no bus service. The only visible amenities were the pub, the church and the village school, standing in a row and faced from the opposite side of the road by the village hall, a telephone kiosk and a letter box.

But now we found out the really important things. The church was threatened with closure on alternate Sundays. It was expensive to run and there was no certainty that the present incumbent would be replaced. Ann made quiet noises indicating her willingness to fight the good fight. She had always been very pro churches but felt that as a new parishioner too much anxiety might sound pushy. I reflected to myself that whatever its spiritual and community merits, the fabric of the church looked obtrusive and out of place. I was not surprised to be told that it had been designed by the same man who produced the Albert Memorial.

It was impressed upon us that the village school was run by a legendary disciplinarian named Miss Fitch. She did not live in the village, but she was of the village. She descended on it each day in term time and administered education to the children of schooling age. We had to understand that an invisible notice was hung over the school door reading 'Parents not admitted'.

We soon found out that the most important of the farms surrounding the village was probably the one owned by Tony. Tony and his wife Diana lived in what was once called 'The Big House'. At any rate the fields opposite the house were referred to deferentially as 'the park'. Tony and Diana were not really 'Big House' people. But the relationship between their house and the village had been established long before they came to live in it. Former occupants of their house had presented the village with that church. Custom required Tony and Diana to be present at every occasion of importance in the village. We gathered that they usually were, but that the occasions which gave them the most obvious pleasure were the cricket matches played on a field maintained by Tony especially for that purpose.

Finally there was Julia. There used to be a forge in the village, but it was now a private house. Julia had lived in it for a long time. Apparently she was the village oracle and knew everything that went on. The time to consult the oracle was on Friday evenings when Julia opened up the room in her house from which she ran the village lending library. During the rest of the week Julia was a painter of wildlife. We were introduced to Julia. Tented in a painter's smock, her legs clad in purple woollen stockings with a hole beginning at one heel and a glass tilted in one hand, Julia surveyed us. In a great deep voice she said slowly, 'So, you have arrived.' The pause between each word was filled with a gusty wheeze. There was rather a lot of Julia inside that paint-smudged smock. The overall effect was immensely dramatic. Every shade of interpretation that could be put on our six months' delay in moving in was there. It was clear to us why Julia and her Friday evening lending library had been described with such affectionate reverence.

# I

# Bagpipes and Lady Jane

We had not been in our new house long before we began to accumulate animals. What other people put into Post Office accounts and holidays, we put into animals and the cost of keeping them. They were all treated as members of the family, and their numbers grew and grew. The freedom we had gained from our move to the house went to our heads. We were all about as bad as each other. But Sue became the ringleader. A gruff little voice saying 'Come and look at . . .', or 'Would it be all right if . . .?' became an increasingly frequent part of the greeting I was given by the family on my return from the office in the evenings.

About the time we were growing out of the guinea-pig

stage and the ramshackle sheds in the garden were full of hutches housing old age pensioners, four-footed, furry and munching their way into a better life, Sue struck up a friendship with one of the families in the village. The mother was artistic, and the father brewed his own beer. They were that sort of family and they kept even more animals than we did, including peacocks. They had a brood of wickedly beautiful children, all girls. They were like long-legged crosses between wild deer and fox cubs. They were enchanting. The youngest daughter Sophie went with C-J to the village school where they were taught by the formid-able Miss Fitch. In term time, Sue would talk C-J into tag-ging on to Sophie after school so that she, Sue, could go down and fetch her. It was not the peacocks that fascinated Sue, it was the bantams. Roaming round the house, in the lane and up by the spring, where the homemade beer was cooled before drinking, was a flock of mongrel bantams, cocks, hens and chicks of all ages. They scratched, clucked and crowed. They ruined the garden. They were every-where.

One summer's day, when she was nearly ten, Sue, freckled, pink and sweaty came bustling into the kitchen clutching two small hen's eggs. She had been assured that she could hatch them out in the airing cupboard and she was going to do it. Into a cardboard box they went, bedded down on cotton wool with an old flannel on top of them. They were turned night and morning and really brooded by that determined small girl. She had a rough idea when things should start to happen and on an eventful evening she heard a faint tapping and a cheep. What followed was calamitous. The shells, and the membranes lining them were too tough for the babies to break. Too late we realized that they were in trouble and broke the eggs open for them. The chicks had spent so much of their stored energy in their efforts to emerge that, although the airing cupboard was amply warm, they both faded away before they had dried out. We all went to bed. Sue had a tight little look on her face that we were all to get to know so well in future years.

Next day two more eggs were started in the airing cupboard. This time Sue sprinkled a few drops of water on the covering flannel each time she turned the eggs. This change in method seemed to do the trick. When the tapping and cheeping started the next time, a little hole soon appeared in each eggshell with a small horny toe prising away at the edge. This time the births were completed without our help. When it was nearing midnight, two bedraggled objects sat weakly on the cotton wool in the box in the airing cupboard – new members of the family. The next morning the picture was quite different. Their fluffy down had dried out and they were round and lively. One was pale yellow and Sue pronounced that it would become a white hen. The other was partridge-coloured and this she was determined would be a cock. They were named Bagpipes and Lady Jane.

Sue set about teaching the new arrivals to eat. Chick crumbs were put in a large box, with a forty-watt lamp hanging above it, and Sue imitated a mother hen's beak, tapping away with the top of a Biro pen. It worked. The chicks learnt to peck at the crumbs. They also learnt that Sue was mother. They lived in their box on top of her chest of drawers. They were smelly, but, as Ann conceded, safe from the cat. They cheeped away, falling silent as soon as they heard someone enter the room. It was always Sue's voice that started the noisiest call for food. When they were old enough to be taken outside they would rush frantically along the garden paths and across the lawn with outstretched beaks and wing stubs flapping, always following the heel of Sue's sandal. Sue never questioned that it was natural to take her chicks for a walk and they never doubted that it was right to follow her. They thrived.

Sue named them well. Lady Jane became a small neat white hen, beautiful, gentle, tame and demure. Bagpipes was clearly a cockerel, stunted and boisterous, wearing a pagan tartan in red, brown and black shot with green. Sue grandly told everybody that he was a game bird. I could never convince myself of this, but certainly whatever he lacked in blood line he made up for in aggression. He grew long spurs and a great red comb that flopped over one eye with a sinister piratical drape.

Bagpipes liked a fight and he took a fierce delight in fighting wellington boots. It was Mark who discovered this. From the time Bagpipes was old enough to raise his hackles, he used to threaten, alternately crouching and mincing, when anything came near the old sheds where he and Lady Jane roosted. His favourite tactic was to wait until the intruder was just past and then attack from the rear with wings, beak and spurs, retiring with a satisfied flap of his wings when the edge of his territory was reached. The cat was terrified of him and the dogs treated him with respect. Mark was wheeling a barrow load of logs past the shed one afternoon when Bagpipes attacked. All Mark could do was either abandon his logs with ignominy or kick out with his boots. He kicked out and Bagpipes persisted with his attack. He was furious and pursued poor Mark well beyond his usual limit. When Mark took his boots off, both had been pierced by Bagpipes's spurs, rubber and fabric as well. Thereafter wellington boots were seen as a challenge, and on wet days it was wise to steer clear of Bagpipes in his prime. He always went for one's legs anyhow, but never with real ferocity unless they were inside wellingtons. Sue was exempt – Bagpipes respected his mother.

Lady Jane gave us many eggs. Too small for breakfast, but just right for Ann to pickle. Through no fault of Bagpipes, Lady Jane's eggs were never fertile. She never had chicks of her own. She was everything the first hen in the family should have been and we missed her when she didn't survive her fourth winter.

I cannot truthfully say that Bagpipes missed Lady Jane, for by the time she died we had given him many other wives whom he trod and guarded with enthusiasm. He was the father of numerous children – many of whom we ate – and the victor in many fights with unwary visitors.

As Bagpipes grew older he mellowed. He actually grew a few white hackles. Despite the rakish angle of his comb he managed to look respectable, but he was too small to achieve a look of real dignity. Underneath it, he was still the randy little mongrel cock who loved to fight with wellingtons. Sometimes when I was up by the feed bins on a summer's day, while his wives were having dust baths and he was bored, I could feel him practically willing me to go and change into my wellington boots. Once I did it, putting an extra pair of socks on inside, and as soon as I re-appeared 'Old Baggies' – as Ann, who was a favourite target of his, called him – came scuttling out of the straw and minced and fluffed round my legs darting in and planting his spurs as I moved my feet away, fluttering back with a raucous cackle when I threatened him. He was a wicked old devil but it was a long time before I discovered that he was a vulgar little peasant as well. His crow was always a bit unusual, rather like a 'cock-a-doodle-do' with the notes upside down, as it were. It wasn't until I heard the record of that wonderful opera *Evita* by Tim Rice and Andrew Lloyd-Webber that I realized Bagpipes's cry of triumph as he saw his victims off was 'Screw the middle classes!' – just as Julie Covington sang it. He was to keep us faithful company through ten eventful years.

The arrival of Bagpipes and Lady Jane had marked the beginning of an attraction to dual-purpose animals. Apart from finding extra wives for Bagpipes, we started to collect recognized breeds – Pekings, Polish, Plymouth Rock, Silkies and many others. We had great fun with the chicks which were all enchanting – particularly the Pekings that hatched complete with sets of downy plus-fours reaching down to their ankles. The point was that these dual-purpose birds gave us small eggs – most of which Ann pickled – and young stock for Sue to sell to the fancy bird market. After some initial hesitation the cull stock went into the pot. At one time Sue had dealings with about every fancier within a thirty-mile radius from us. She also acquired a vast number of antique chicken houses – most of them free of charge from people glad to clear their land. Some of those houses were so decrepit that their inmates wandered in and out at will. This led to excitement at egg collection time. The hens seemed to lay almost anywhere except in their nesting boxes. Ann and Sue soon smelt out every laying place and scampered round the garden with wooden trugs shouting gleefully to one another as they uncovered the hidden harvest each afternoon. Sue's school friends and Ann's teatime guests were pressed into helping. They enjoyed it, but word soon got round that we practically allowed our undisciplined chickens to live with us.

One of our specialities resulted from an attempt to produce, by crossing Old English game bantams and the much bigger Andalusians, a bird with small neat hackles of a deep steely blue. Such feathers would be prized by fishermen – like me – who tie their own trout flies. We never got the colour we wanted, but we did produce a very even strain of small pale grey birds which were prolific layers – more small eggs for pickling. This particular strain were all named after flowers. The most striking of them – a nice little hen – was called Snapdragon. Eventually larger birds laying larger eggs joined us, but for a time Ann practically lived on pickled eggs. The rest of us got heartily sick of them.

# 2

# Henry

Henry was a Chinese goose – or rather gander. Chinese geese are a beautiful breed. They are medium sized as geese go, with unusually long and slender necks. The over-all impression is one of sleekness. Their colouring is a subtle combination of browns, fawn and cream set off by orange feet and a black bill. A breed characteristic is a dark colour streak extending laterally from the knob at the top of the bill to the rear of the eye. This gives them a particularly intelligent look. They have easy going temperaments, mix well with children and are an ideal dual-purpose bird for decoration and egg production. They are said to make good table birds, with more of the lean dark flesh of wild geese on them and less of the farmyard goose's fat. They are also excellent lawnmowers. We found they could be trusted to roam free in the garden and that it was only the grass that was nibbled close. Their droppings were a green, slimy, numerous nuisance, but at an early stage in our more extensive involvement with animals we had built the 'Dirt Lock'.

The Dirt Lock was a small room we had tacked on to the outside of the house so that the back door opened into it. Anybody coming into the house from the garden or animal areas was supposed to come through the Dirt Lock, shedding boots and wet clothing on the way. Theoretically any animal with access to the house was supposed to be let in the same way, after inspection. The next room in from the Dirt Lock housed the boiler and was a haven for wet, but – hopefully – clean cats and dogs. Despite the ingenuity of the animals, including non-house animals, in wheedling the children into letting them into the house by other routes, the arrangement worked pretty well.

We had bought Henry, together with his wife Patsy, as a breeding pair from a dealer in Sussex. Shortly after they were joined by Blue, a stocky common or garden brown and white farmyard goose which one of the girls had acquired somehow. We were all so easily tempted to pick up animals at the slightest excuse that newcomers arrived with bewildering speed. Normally the first ceremony was to give them a name. Sue was the official namer of all animals joining the family, and she never forgot who they were. Even when the resident chicken population had risen to something near fifty she knew the name of every laying bird and stud cockerel. At one time I held the disgraceful record of being the only member of the family who had ever disposed of an animal. I had lost the cat to my sister-in-law in a poker game. I was forgiven eventually. We lived in a tiny flat in London at the time and Sung – who was a Siamese cat – was far better off down in the country.

The main egg flow from Patsy and Blue started in early

spring. But this was preceded by the mating season. Not many male birds have got very obvious means of making love. Ganders are among the privileged few and in the case of Henry the means, when in use, was orange and ostentatious. In early March, Henry would manoeuvre Patsy and Blue towards a large chipped enamel bowl which served as a drinking trough for them near the wood shed. His opening move was to get into the bowl, flap his wings, splash about and display generally, giving forth great meaningful honks from time to time. He would then get out of the bowl, waggle his tail and look hopefully at the other two. It was usually some days before Patsy – it was always Patsy first – stepped delicately into the bowl, raised her tail and lowered her head, pretending to drink. Henry needed no second invitation and, with great splashings as Patsy strove to keep her balance, Henry was on her back tupping away and honking his cries of triumphant male superiority. It looked more like colourful rape than lovemaking. We were to see the affectionate side of their relationship much later. Why the mating always took place in the drinking bowl I am not quite sure. I can only suppose that, in their wild origins, these geese mated in the reedy shallows at lake edges, but the possible significance of this in the evolutionary process has always eluded me. Perhaps it was just Henry being eccentric.

Some observers have claimed that geese are amongst those birds that, whatever the temptation, are monogamous and pair for life. These three were an exception to this rule. Henry mated with Blue as well. But I am convinced that her role was not that of wife. She was an official concubine approved of by Patsy. When Henry was in the mood, it was always Patsy who stepped into the bowl first. Blue would only be invited into the bowl, with Patsy looking on, some twenty minutes later. On one, never to be forgotten occasion, Blue, in an agony of frustration, stepped into the bowl uninvited. Ann was showing some polite, but unenthusiastic visitors the animal quarters at the time. Lovemaking by those three geese of ours was always noisy, spectabular and unusual. Henry, who suffered no inhibitions, answered Blue's tail wagging with a 'If that's what you want you can have it' display of awesome, powerful, prolonged and penetrating vigour. Ann could not get her visitors back to the house fast enough.

When the two geese started laying – an egg each, every other day – one egg was sufficient to make an enormous saffron-coloured omelette – the trio were always moved into the 'Frog'. The Frog is the name of a large enclosure on the north side of the house which contains a huge mound of ragstone boulders and greensand running three-quarters of the length of the house and rising to eave height at its top. Sizeable trees grow on this mound. In the winter, when the leaves are down, it looks, when viewed from the top of the cliff to its north, just like a large squat frog. The Frog is a mixed blessing. It provides a number of our animals with an interesting home and nesting places for wrens and robins. Field mice live on it and it also protects the house. There are some very large rocks in the cliff face which will come loose one day and, when they do, it is only the Frog which will prevent them thundering down the hill, leaving a big hole in our house on the way. On the other hand it acts as a natural water reservoir and the wall of the house at its nearest point to the Frog is always damp. More building society problems.

One spring Patsy went broody. 'Pregerant' C-J called it, which we took to mean pregnancy through ignorance. Blue never became 'pregerant'. Concubines have more wisdom in these matters. Patsy took us quite unawares for she stopped laying and Blue came out on strike in sympathy. We only had three goose eggs in the house for Patsy to brood. It so happened they were all her own eggs. Patsy moved into a small dog kennel at the base of the Frog and, watched by a solicitous Henry, built her nest. Straw and old fern fronds made up the bulk of it and when she started to line it with down plucked from her creamy breast, we put the three eggs under her.

The events of the next weeks were fascinating. Inspired by the urge to protect and hatch her eggs, Patsy built her nest high up round her adding more down lining all the while and frequently working over it keeping it neat and snug. We never saw her leave the nest the whole time she was sitting. We kept a water bowl full within her reach and she drank, but showed no interest in coming to corn or grass. From time to time she would half rise from her eggs and, making full use of her long sinuous neck, take her head and beak down past her legs into the warm depths of the nest to turn her eggs. But the most wonderful thing to see was the behaviour of Henry. Blue had retired tactfully to the other end of the enclosure and kept some guinea-fowl company. Henry never strayed far from Patsy snugged down in the kennel. When Patsy reached out for a drink, Henry would step quietly to the front of her and lower his head with a quiet affectionate hiss – quite different from an angry hiss. Patsy would respond and for a few moments they would touch and caress each other's extended and curved necks with their beaks. It was a delicate ballet in slow motion cream and brown. Now we saw Henry in the role of an affectionate lover. He was also rather fierce and anyone straying too near Patsy was threatened, with the menace of real attack showing through very clearly. Attack by a full grown Chinese gander would be no fun for anyone.

After some weeks all the eggs hatched and Patsy had three beautiful golden-brown goslings. Sadly one of them had a badly displaced hip joint and had to be put down. It was no easy task to take it from under the eyes of Patsy and Henry, both of whom were devoted guardians. The other two grew quickly and it was not long before they were big enough to climb to the top of the Frog with their parents. A public footpath runs between the Frog and the cliff foot and, on sunny weekends in early summer that year, the goose family always attracted onlooking groups of all ages.

By the end of the summer one of the youngsters had been sold to a home in Wales. The other, a nice young goose, was kept and named Penny. All the grass on the Frog had disappeared and we were feeding the geese and guinea-fowl on corn and the occasional trugful of grass and weeds from the vegetable garden. It was time to take the geese down to the paddock to feed up on grass before the winter.

# 3

# Fox Trouble

The ridge is heavily populated with wild animals  Roe deer, badgers and foxes are the largest of our wild neighbours. Squirrels, all kinds of mice, voles and shrews, stoats, weasels, a large rabbit population and all manner of birds live round us as well. Julia knows where to find them all. The ridge is her outdoor studio. The sketches she makes on her early morning expeditions are worked up into finished pictures back in her home in the village. Before we put up rabbit netting, badgers used to come on to our land and rake out wasp nests from the terrace banks and scoff the rough white grubs. The badgers are good neighbours. The foxes are bad neighbours. The roe deer are very shy and we catch occasional glimpses of them only either late at night in car headlights or when we are going through the woods during the day on horseback.

I have lived in the country, on and off, for a large part of my life, but the scream of a vixen calling to attract the dog foxes in midwinter still sets my senses tingling in a strangely disturbing way. It is not possible to describe the call. It is wild and compelling. While one half of me wants the noise to stop, the other half wills the call to be repeated. There are many foxes round us and on a still frosty night in January or early February you can be sure of hearing the vixens from the cliff above us, the woods around us, and, particularly, the fields below us.

The more vixens we hear calling in winter, the more cubs will be born near us in early spring and heavy cubbing years mean trouble. The rabbit population around us now consists mainly of a strain breeding above ground and resistant to myxomatosis. As the rabbit population has increased, so the drift of the fox population back from the outer London suburbs near us has accelerated. When one talks of this drift, many people think of daring parties of foxes crossing scores of main roads. It is true that many foxes are killed on the roads each year, but I am convinced that an even greater number use the uninterrupted highway created by the railway to travel between the country and the suburbs. During the time that the countryside was almost denuded of rabbits, I saw foxes raiding dustbins in the Old Kent Road in the small hours of the morning and from an early morning train I have seen quite young cubs in the vicinity of Lewisham.

Although the local hunt can keep the fox population within reasonable bounds on the flat weald to the south of us, they have no effect on the population on the ridge. It is a natural wildlife sanctuary and its steeper cliffs, near vertical and a mixture of sand and fissured white ragstone, are unassailable by dog or man. It is in these cliffs that many of our foxes have their earths, coming out to hunt by night and returning in the early dawn. It is only when the cubs are at their most demanding that we see foxes by daylight.

Although finally we have come to fear them, we have always found the foxes fascinating. A fox track runs along a narrow sandy ledge traversing the cliff behind the house. A nearby earth always holds cubs in spring and sometimes we see the dog fox or the vixen padding quickly across the cliff face with a field mouse or other juicy gobbet to give the cubs. One year the vixen sat on the ledge with four fluffy innocent cubs quivering with curiosity in our full view, watching us as we watched them, for a full half hour. The vixen knew they were quite safe – we had no shotgun at the time – and we were sure that the incident was part of the cubs' education. We could practically hear the vixen saying, 'Those are people – don't get too close to them.' 'Those are dogs – always break your scent when you hear them behind you.' 'Those are chickens – we will teach you how to take them in a week or so.' 'Those are guinea-fowl – keep out of their sight when we are hunting – they are alarm raisers.' And so on.

The year Penny – our young goose – was born, and the year before that, were heavy cubbing years. If two heavy years occur together, the second year, with a high fox population and increased competition for food, is very bad for farmers and people like us. In the first of those years there was trouble at lambing time.

There are two farms below us which run sheep – Tony's and a smaller one. Tony's ewes are brought in at lambing time and only let out again when the lambs are strong enough on their legs. It is only a matter of a day or two. On the other farm windbreaks of hurdles and straw bales are placed near the hedges for the ewes to lamb unattended. This is a perfectly usual way of arranging matters, particularly on a small farm which is short-handed. The snag about it is that, with some of the heavier, more highly bred sheep, the lambs are terribly vulnerable to fox attack in the hours immediately after birth. This is all too often the case with the first of twin lambs, when the ewe is in labour producing the other one.

On the first of those two years, lambing started in February on both farms. The farm with the outdoor lambing system had lamb losses night after night. One of the sickening things about foxes is that when they are not at full stretch killing for their cubs they will kill for sport. In February the cubs are not yet born. The vixens are fattening up in preparation for their youngsters, but the dog foxes are bored. I am sure that it is the dog foxes that are the worst culprits in the case of February lambs. Time after time on a February morning I have seen the skinny little corpses with torn throats lying in the field with the puzzled and distraught ewes trying to nose them to their feet. Very probably only one lamb would have been taken for food – the rest were the victims of a savage bloodlust. The same phenomenon occurs occasionally with loose dogs raiding sheep flocks and killing the adult sheep. With lambs the culprits are always foxes, or nearly always.

The only thing to do in these circumstances is to bring the flock in, if there is covered space or an easily protected fold available, and launch a counter-attack on the foxes with trap and gun. The trouble with traps is the risk of catching innocent prowlers – especially cats. The more exacting, but better way is to stake a couple of string bags of gamey chicken guts out in a field, known to be visited by foxes, some ten yards in front of a field shelter. If there is no field shelter, straw bales will do just as well. A powerful torch, a twelve-bore shotgun, a sharp ear and a good eye and willingness to stay up all night will do the rest. If someone will keep you company and shine the torch when squashy noises are heard in front, so much the better. The farmer who was suffering the losses shot a number of foxes that year and strung them up on a barbed-wire fence as a deterrent. The local paper photographed the grisly row and there were soon squawks of protest. That farmer had my complete sympathy. Some people argue that the sight and smell of the rotting corpses simply attract more foxes and are not deterrents at all. They may be right, but I understood the farmer's urge to try anything. I had seen what the foxes had done to his lambs. He could not afford the losses – no farmer could. The rest of us and many of the other wild animals could not afford the consequences of an uncontrolled explosion of the fox population.

That year we lost some ducks. We had bought young Aylesburys for fattening – the technique is to plump them up quickly and kill them while they are still downy and their second feathers haven't yet sprouted. They were in a portable run on the lawn below the house where we could keep an eye on them. But that run could be up-ended. We lost all six one night in early June. It was not a matter of bloodlust – they had been taken for cub food. As likely as not the cubs had been involved in the raid. We searched the boundaries and found one tell-tale bit of white down in the hedge at the bottom of the paddock. Early next morning, Mark went out with a twelve-bore and his hunt terrier to investigate the copse below a neighbour's garden about a half-mile down the hill. The terrier put up a big dog fox and Mark shot it. He was walking jauntily back home swinging the fox by its brush, when he came face to face with our neighbour, dressing-gowned, sleepy-eyed and furious. He had bought a cine camera especially for the purpose of filming the fox family in that copse. We smothered our neighbours with apologies for days. We felt awful. But those foxes had eaten our ducks!

The next year was really bad. There were losses from the lambing flocks as far away as three miles from the ridge. More desiccated fox corpses appeared on the barbed-wire fences. This time the local newspaper left the matter alone and we were spared the curious coming out to gawk. The foxes hit us in April. The first to suffer were the hens. Any hen running loose was liable to go missing, by night or by day. The foxes were very clever and silent. They were hardly ever spotted by us or by the dogs. We took the hint and put all the hens into houses. Around one house we fenced in a run, enclosing it in a high floppy fence of chicken wire. A dozen birds in full lay were put into a large portable house with nesting boxes accessible from the rear. We gave those birds deep litter and no run. They were all taken in one night. Somehow the foxes got in by way of the nesting boxes. The weight and height of the timber hatch over the nesting boxes was such that it could only have been done by two foxes working together – one wedging the hatch open with its body while the other got in. Taking the hens out one by one would have been no problem. The next day hysterical barking by Mark's terrier brought Ann rushing to an upstairs window. The dog was racing towards the hen run where a big dog fox was bouncing up and down, leaping and twisting, trying to reach the top of the chicken netting. It shot off with the terrier about a yard behind it and nipped up and over the chain-link boundary fence.

One Cuckoo Maran hen had a lucky escape that spring. She had been missing a day when she turned up on the footpath outside the house. She was walking slowly and unsteadily with her head skewed over to one side as if her neck was dislocated. It was only stiff. She must have been carried by the neck up into the earth in the cliffs and then escaped somehow. We brought her into the warm and slowly she recovered, stiff neck and all. That old bird is still with us.

The next to go were all but one of the flock of laying ducks. The ducks were Khaki Campbells. A white drake kept them company. It was just that and no more. He had no male instincts whatsoever. He was called Omo. The name went well with his colour and purity of mind. I had taken two weeks off from the office to do some tidying up on our land. It was the end of May.

Ducks make an awful mess of a run. In no time it is paddled down into a slippery squittery mess. It was a nice day and I was on the spot, so we let the ducks out. They waddled around quacking happily. Up to the house they went and back again. I watched them for a time. A large piece of black plastic sheeting lay on the ground nearby and Omo led them to it, lowered his bill and started to drink it. The rest tried to splash in it. They thought it was water. I have seen swallows and house martins make the same mistake with wheel-polished tarmac in midsummer, alighting on the black road surface and trying to pick up what their senses have told them should be wet mud. I stopped watching the ducks and went on with my work. After about an hour I realized everything was strangely quiet. There was a noise missing. It was the noise of quiet contented quacking. Slightly uneasy, I went to investigate a scrub-covered bank about twenty yards away, which lay in the direction of the last quacks I could remember. There was not a sign of the ducks anywhere. I called Ann and we searched the whole area, urgently and thoroughly. We were just giving up in despair when we heard a quiet familiar noise. Crouched under a bush, flat on the ground and looking up at us with a trusting brown eye was the sole survivor. The rest had been taken in broad daylight, within twenty yards of me, without a sound of protest. It must have been a raid by a complete fox family. How foxes manage to silence their victims so effectively I have often wondered, but they do. We took the surviving duck up to the Frog, where it had the geese and guinea-fowl for company.

The following morning I left home about eight o'clock to go riding. As I stepped out of the house a fox yapped. From the depth of the voice, I knew it was a dog fox.

It was very close – somewhere up the cliff. The yap was a signal of some kind – perhaps that I was leaving the property. I had the feeling of being treated with complete contempt. When I returned, Ann was bristling with indignation and near to tears – 'Bloody foxes,' she said. Shortly after I had left, the guinea-fowl had set up a great chattering and cackling. This was not so unusual – they challenged every passerby in this way. But soon they were joined by an outburst of squawking and quacking that was different. Ann had rushed into the garden with a broom in time to see the remaining duck being chased all over the heather bed alongside the Frog by a fox. The fox kept it up until the last moment before Ann got there. With the fox gone, the duck, which had brought the trouble on itself by somehow getting under the enclosure wire, collapsed exhausted at Ann's feet. Her quacking had saved her and we renamed her Quackers.

The rest of that summer was quiet and in the autumn the four geese were taken down to the paddock where there was a nice crop of green September grass. One morning Blue was missing. It could only have been a fox and we cursed ourselves for not shutting them up at night. We lugged a big Noah's ark down the garden and tipped it over the paddock rails. Each night the geese were shut up and each morning let out by Sue or C-J before they went to school. One Sunday in October I let them out myself at about nine o'clock on my way to my horse. I was back at ten thirty and was met by an anxious family. The geese were missing. Henry, Patsy and Penny had all been taken by foxes in those one and a half hours. We found feathers where they had struggled in the grass and more feathers in the hedge. If only they had called for help – but they had struggled in silence. We will never forget that year. We have never replaced the ducks and geese.

# 4

# Moon and Sixpence

The paddock at the bottom of the garden is long and narrow. It is not big – about a third of an acre, but it is nicely sheltered by surrounding trees and a high hazel hedge runs along the bottom edge keeping the south-westerly gales out. Jays nest in the hazel hedge and each year a large conical May tree at one end of the hedge is home for a pair of magpies who raise an incredible number of youngsters in their snug, domed nest. When the youngsters fly you wonder how so many could have been packed in so little space. By the time one is down to the paddock one is on to the clay, and flatter and softer land – easier on the feet, but very slippery in wet weather. The paddock was strongly enclosed with oak post and rail fencing before we came to the house. Because they are embedded in clay, the oak uprights sometimes come very loose in dry weather as the sockets shrink away from them.

One evening in midsummer, still in my office clothes, I was lured down to the paddock by the suggestion that the fencing needed inspection as a matter of urgency. With a grinning family behind me, I was confronted by two shaggy-coated brown and white animals, standing about two feet high at the shoulder, eyeing me suspiciously and looking something like a cross between sheep and goats, with long tails. They were two Jacob sheep – shearling ewes – one year old that is – and their names were Moon and Sixpence.

We had been thinking of venturing into sheep for some time. Ann and the two girls had followed up an advertisement in the local paper, found a flock of Jacobs and bought the two ewes on the spot. It was not just a matter of impulse. Jacobs are good dual-purpose sheep. There is a strong demand for them as park animals, and they are excellent eating. They are a hardy breed, and first generation crosses with other breeds produce vigorous meaty lambs.

We had read recently that a Scottish farmer had paid some hundreds of pounds for a Jacob ram. Scottish farmers don't spend that sort of money lightly.

I was a bit apprehensive about Moon and Sixpence. They were the largest farm creatures we had acquired yet and they were very different from my idea of sheep. However, I confined myself to the comment that the paddock had been fenced with horses and ponies in mind and that I didn't see what was to prevent the ewes from simply stepping over the bottom rail and raiding the garden. Ann and C-J withdrew discreetly leaving Sue to explain to me that generations of breeding had taught sheep to respect fences and that even if they did stray in a fit of absent-mindedness, they would behave just like the geese and only eat grass. At any rate, that was the gist of it.

Apparently generations of breeding had taught Moon and Sixpence a great deal. Whenever I was about, they were grazing innocently in the middle of the paddock. But strange things were happening in the garden. Small shrubs were disappearing, eaten down to the ground. Larger shrubs and trees were being barked by something. Whatever was doing it had a particular liking for the camellias. That demonstrated excellent taste, but did not fill me with enthusiasm. I asked Sue if she was quite sure the two ewes were not getting out. Sue said she was quite sure with a 'don't you dare disagree with me' quality in her voice. Rather less belligerently she pointed out there was no sign of sheep droppings and that the tree barking stopped six inches above ground level. These observations were difficult to counter. The fact remained that the happenings had started as soon as the sheep had arrived.

One morning a full bladder had me out of bed at daybreak. As I was making my rather bug-eyed way back to bed, I looked out of the window. Moon was on the lawn and Sixpence was on one of the shrub beds, nose down and nibbling her way round the stem of a young and highly prized camellia. I shot down the stairs and out on to the path above the lawn. They must have started running as they heard me open the outside door. I was just in time to see them making a guilty hop over the lower paddock rail on their way back in. When I reached the paddock myself they were in the middle standing stock-still looking at me disdainfully. They plainly thought it was a game of grandmother's footsteps and that they were safe as long as they didn't move.

For a short while it was clear that Sue was toying with telling me I was imagining things, but faced with an ultimatum if she did not succeed in confining her darlings to the paddock, she appeared later that day with two long chains and a pair of iron tethering posts and rings. I am not sure where she got them from. From an early age she had the habit of collecting things that might come in useful one day.

All went well for some weeks and then I came home one evening to a sad family. Moon had been found dead during the day. The vet had conducted a quick post-mortem, but there was no apparent cause of death. The ewe was perfectly healthy. Looking back, Ann remembered that Moon had wrapped her tether round a young broom bush and this had left her with a very short lead. I am sure, in the light of our later experience, that Moon had died from heart failure caused by fright in the same way that sheep sometimes do if they get caught up in brambles.

Sixpence was removed from the paddock and tethered in a completely clear field with an old pony nicknamed – not properly named – by the girls as Tubby. The pony belonged to my sister-in-law who lived half a mile from us through the woods. Sixpence and Tubby became great friends and that was to come in very useful.

That autumn we bought three more Jacobs. There were two ewes that Sue named Bramble and Tiger Lily – a rather exotic combination I thought – and a magnificent shearling ram Sue named Orion.

Jacob sheep are either twin-horned or multi-horned. The commonest arrangement on the multi-horned heads is for one pair of horns to curve out and down and round towards the lower jaw and for another pair to twist – it is a twist and not a spiral – upwards and either backwards or forwards. Sometimes there is another pair, a third pair, curving downwards or upwards and occasionally – as in the case of Sixpence – a lopsided arrangement with a twin branched horn on one side and a single horn on the other. The ewes' horns are small and rather slender. The rams' horns are stout and strong and in my opinion, in the case of multi-horned sheep, rather ugly. In the case of twin-horned heads, the ewes have a slender pair twisting upwards and back and outwards, the rams have a magnificent pair curving back and down and round and forward again, just like Landseer drawings of some of the big Scottish sheep. The growth rings give an attractive wrinkled appearance to these rams' horns which are coloured a dark blackish brown and a deep olive yellow. Orion had a fine pair. Bramble and Tiger Lily had twin-horned heads as well.

Before the arrival of these three, we had put two strands of fencing wire round the paddock above and below the bottom rail. It worked well for about a week. Then Orion got bored. He jumped the top rail and the ewes followed. I was watching when it happened and could hardly believe my eyes. Orion simply trotted lightly up the slope, stood off and leapt. He cleared the top rail – some three feet high – by a good foot. The ewes could not manage that height, but they scrambled through the gap between the top rail and the upper wire strand.

The next six weeks were an awful sort of nightmare. First the sheep started to devastate the garden. They browsed their way through everything. I remember the sickening empty feeling as I watched Sixpence pull up a complete patch of hoop petticoat daffodils which were showing their thin tubular leaves in the alpine garden and suck them down like green spaghetti. And of course, the more we chased them off the flower beds, the wilder they became.

All we could do was to keep cool and systematically plan our revenge and the sheep's recapture. We bought some rolls of stout rectangular sheep netting, borrowed a wire strainer from a sympathetic Tony, and started doing what we should have done to begin with. The matter was urgent. There was no guarantee that Orion would not get bored with the garden as well and take off in earnest. The thought of the ridge populated with our Jacob sheep was not at all appealing. We reckoned that if the ewes could not escape from the paddock, Orion would not jump out and leave them.

The work had to be done as soon as the netting had been bought. That meant working in the dark after I got home from the office. Mark was away at school, C-J was growing fast and needed her sleep, so that left Ann, Sue and me. We worked flat out for three evenings. The weather was foul and much of the paddock's outer perimeter was brambly. Ann held the torch, I unrolled the netting and hammered home the fencing staples and Sue worked the wire strainer. When any kind of stiff wire is uncoiled it does surprising things, particularly when it is wet. That netting behaved like Old Nick himself. The clay was greasy with the rain, the ground was uneven and the brambles particularly prickly. We finished the job at midnight on the third night and we hadn't sworn at each other once. That in itself was a fair indication that we all recognized a real crisis.

The next job was to catch the sheep. They were pretty flighty and we could get nowhere near them in daytime. We didn't dare press the chase too hard. The woods and the cliff looked horribly inviting. We resorted to low cunning. Sixpence had learned to associate Sue rattling a bucket of pony nuts with food. Most sheep are greedy and these were no exception. For a couple of days Sue rattled the bucket of nuts in a small spinney at one corner of the grounds and, when she saw the sheep approaching – the ewes led by Sixpence, Orion bringing up the rear – would spill the nuts on the ground and walk away. One evening after dark we concealed ourselves in the bushes and Sue rattled her bucket. The sheep sensed something was wrong but they didn't quite know what. Eventually they filed hesitatingly past our hiding place. At a pre-arranged signal from me, we sprang the ambush, jumping from our cover and clutching for those rank smelling shaggy fleeces. It was a disaster. Leaping sheep exploded in every direction and vanished into the darkness. This time we did swear at each other.

For the next two nights we tried a variety of round-up techniques. It was no good. The sheep were very quick, very quiet and very clever. Even the moon did not help. Their patch patterned coats were perfect camouflage.

I was the only one who came near to them and that was by accident. I was sitting on the ground at the top of the garden, taking a breather, when the little flock passed silently by in Indian file. They merged quietly into the shadows cast by some bushes and stood still. They were listening to Sue shouting to Ann – they were both at the far end of the garden – 'I know they are in this bit some-where.' Ann was clearing her throat, her usual signal of disbelieving tetchiness.

The next night Orion jumped out. We were near enough to see him go. Tiger Lily scrambled after him. Bramble and Sixpence dithered and thought better of it. Sue let out a great wail of despair, 'My God, Tony will never forgive me.' Sue did have something to worry about – we all did. Many of the neighbouring flocks were in lamb and the rams had been removed long since. What the effect of Orion on the rampage might be did not bear thinking about.

Tony had been very good to Sue. He gave her orphan lambs to rear at lambing time and did his best to quench her growing thirst for farming knowledge. Tony and Diana bred Arab horses on the farm. Sue plainly had her eye on them for future work possibilities. I suspected Tony and Diana had an eye on Sue for the same reason. To the amusement of the rest of us, Sue insisted on controlling our relationship with the pair of them.

Luckily the next day was Saturday and I could devote myself to sheep and not to the office. Orion and Tiger Lily

42

were in a large field beside and slightly downhill of us. There was no point in the bucket technique. Mark was home for the weekend, and, strung out across the field, we all advanced on the two fugitives. Orion promptly jumped the barbed-wire fence surrounding the field and vanished into the woods. Tiger Lily tried to follow and got stuck in the brambles. We all fell upon her. I half frog-marched, and half rode that ewe all the way back to the paddock. It was the only way to get her there. I got astride her and held her horns while Sue encouraged with the occasional twisting of her tail from behind. In between frog-marching, we proceeded with great bounds as Tiger Lily leapt into the air. Although I had her by the horns, the insides of my thighs were bruised and scraped from the horn tips digging in.

We forgot about Orion for the moment and turned our attention to Bramble and Sixpence. We decided on another ambush. Remarkably, Sue was able to re-establish confidence in the corner spinney with her bucket technique. We remembered the leaping and this time we draped and strung some old herring netting I had bought some years before – with a fruit cage in mind – through the bushes. It was a sort of funnel trap with the nuts at the top end and the ewes' line of approach at the wider bottom end. When we sprang the trap, I grabbed Bramble who was caught up in the herring net. Ann and Sue collided with one another. Sixpence escaped.

With Bramble and Tiger Lily reunited in the paddock, Sue had a bright idea. Sixpence felt lost and alone and was being very noisy about it. We knew exactly where she was, bleating anxiously and running up and down by the top boundary fence. We were only thankful that she could not jump as well as Orion. We knew he was out there in the darkness somewhere. Sue went and fetched Tubby the pony and led her along the footpath outside the boundary fence.

As she passed the small top wicket gate she opened it. Sixpence, producing deep affectionate baas now, came through the top gate and followed the old pony all the way round the outside of the grounds and in again through the paddock gate. We breathed a sigh of relief and left the pony in the paddock to help settle them all down. At least we had got the three ewes back.

# 5

# Wayward Moon Shadow

Orion was still very much at large and enjoying it. The whole village knew about it. We found it only too easy to imagine what was being said in Julia's lending library on Friday nights. The day after the three Jacob ewes had been re-enfolded in the paddock, Orion found one of the neighbouring flocks of sheep. It was not one of the nearest flocks, but one about a half-mile to the west of us, in a steeply sloping field with woodland bordering it on two sides. We were telephoned by an excited farmer who had seen Orion leap into the field from the woods and step delicately towards the flock calling them imperiously with his great horned head held high. Apparently the flock had obeyed the call with such enthusiasm that the sheep netting had been flattened and the bordering woods filled with in-lamb ewes, who ought to have known better, surging after their new master across the carpet of old leaves under the oak trees and into the deep thickets of coppiced chest-nut. It had taken the farmer, his family and his dogs some four hours to separate the ewes from Orion, drive them back into the field and re-erect the fencing. That done he had telephoned us. He had no hesitation in deciding whom to contact. To ordinary farmers Jacob sheep look most unusual. We were the only family in the neighbourhood known to keep unusual animals of that size.

That farmer was kind and polite but firm. We had let Orion out, so to speak, and it was up to us to get him back again. At least we knew where to start looking. We con-tacted everyone in the area, explained our predicament and asked them to telephone us if they caught sight of him. Should they also be able to shut him in their garage so much the better, but please, no one was to take any chances. We did not want to overemphasize the possible dangers, but we were a little worried. From the garden episodes we knew a bit about Orion. There was precious little chance of his being cornered, but if he was – well, he weighed about seven stone and could accelerate from nought to some twenty-five miles per hour over five yards, threatening with a colossal boss where his horns sprouted from his head. In addition those horns could be used with a wicked hooking action. We didn't want anyone hurt and my Householders Comprehensive did not stretch to such risks.

The messages came flooding in. Orion was very mobile. He was also very attracted to that flock of sheep. His taste of power as leader had gone to his head. Two days after the first episode, he took that flock into the woods with him again. This time the farmer was not so polite. Ann scurried from sighting to sighting. She had not a hope of catching him, but, if she could keep contact, it would give me a better chance when the weekend came round. Unfortunately, Mark was away again for the time being.

The weekend came round with a vengeance. I spent two days engaged in violent cross-country running. It was no contest. That ram was very fast with immense endurance. Sometimes he would let me get within fifty yards of him and would leap over the nearest fence and run to the next vantage point on his circuit. If there was already a fence or hedge between us, he was quite content to let me within ten yards – never much nearer – while he snatched a nibble or so of grass – refuelling – watching me with one eye. He worked me on a large circle of about four miles' diameter with its circumference running obligingly through woods, across streams, paths and fields, uphill, downhill. It was hell. At the end of that weekend I was a lot lighter and Orion knew he had me taped.

For the first two days of the next week there were no sightings. We wondered what devilment the evil beast would get up to next. He did not leave us in suspense for long. On the third day we got a call from Tony. Orion had been trying his leadership techniques with one of his flocks. Fortunately Tony's fences were made to keep in bullocks and horses and Orion had flitted off when he had seen Tony coming to investigate the cause of the excitement. Sue started cussing. That was usual. The animals were normally the last to be blamed.

He kept to himself on the Thursday – probably browsing in the depths of the woods with the roe deer. On the Friday, a housewife, who had come out to the country in her car to collect sweet chestnuts from where they lay on the ground, had a nasty shock. She drove her car off the road into the edge of the woods and got out to start her gathering. She found herself face to face with Orion, gazing at her with baleful black and yellow eyes beneath flicking ears and those heavy curling horns. She shot into her car, dropping the ignition key on the ground. She swore to her friends afterwards that Orion had kept her pinned down, lowering his head every time she opened the car door, to retrieve the key, for three hours. I wonder. However, news was getting around in a circle wider than the village that a large animal was on the loose in the woods on the ridge. Things were getting serious.

The next weekend and chasing time came round again. I assumed Orion would use the same circle and posted the girls at strategic points. With Orion well in the lead on the first circuit, I reversed direction, got into the car and drove like Jehu to intercept him on the other side. Orion made his first mistake. He had trotted cheerfully past C-J, who had held her ground, when he saw me advancing on him. Instead of jumping into the next field, he ducked into the forecourt of the nearest house. A startled car washer had the presence of mind to shut the gates, and we had him. On one side was the house. The other three sides consisted of a high ragstone wall with a single gate into the garden and a large double one out on to the drive. I leant over the double gates – shouted 'thank you' to a rapidly closing front door and leered at Orion. Orion looked at me thoughtfully, turned, took three quick steps and cleared the garden gate. I measured that gate afterwards. It stood a full five feet.

That was the end of the running. We would have to find someone with a rifle and tranquilliser darts. You cannot find people like that so easily. I had to wait until the Monday when I could ask someone at the London Zoo. They were very helpful, and gave me a telephone number in East Kent. Before I could try it, Ann telephoned me at the office. Orion had reappeared with one of Tony's flocks and this time Tony had shot him with a rifle. He was quite right of course.

The big question was – had Orion covered the ewes? Jacobs have such long shaggy fleeces that you cannot be sure of pregnancy until you see their udders bagging

48

up. That's all very well if the ewe will stand still enough for you to look. Our ewes were not keen on standing still for long when we were about. We did not want to risk any disaster catching them up, so we just waited and hoped. In late March, Sue was thrilled to find Sixpence with a new-born single ram lamb. Jacob lambs are superb. The coat colours are a creamy white with patches and spots of a deep brown. In unshorn adult sheep the sun and rain fade this brown to a mid-chocolate. In shorn adults and new-born lambs it shows a glossy black in reflected light and a ruddy brown only in transmitted light. Just like black cattle in fact. The difference with the lambs is that the white is more white than cream. The combination of these gleaming white and glossy black patches is enchanting. Their heads are pretty too. Many lambs look plain stupid with an imbecilic fixed grin – the lambs of Romney Marsh sheep for example. Jacob lambs have heads like small intelligent calves. This similarity to miniature cattle is quite startling. The similarity stops with the tail though. Jacobs are allowed to keep their tails so you get the full effect of those excited little black and white catkins wiggling away as the lambs suckle, knees down, bottoms up.

Bramble and Tiger Lily also produced single ram lambs. They were nice, but Sixpence's son was a beauty, with regular markings on his legs and face. Sue named him Moon Shadow in memory of his aunt. She had registered the prefix Wayward (shades of Orion!) with the Jacob sheep society and so his full name was Wayward Moon Shadow. He was Shadow for short of course. He was an adventurous fellow, easily the cheekiest of the three. Lambs start grazing early in their lives. At first it is a matter of supplementing mother's milk, but by the time they are weaned in the autumn it is the other way about. It did not take Shadow long to learn how to creep through the rectangular netting stapled to the paddock fence and graze the sweeter, greener grass on the other side. The other two did not follow his example. It was fun on a summer's evening to wander down to the paddock and watch a naughty little black and white bottom twanging its way back through the wire. Sixpence was a very good mother and when Shadow was out of the paddock she was never far from the fence.

Shadow was kept to become the foundation sire of our Jacob flock. The other two were sold in Ashford market for twelve pounds each that autumn. Quite a good price we thought. They were not good enough to sell to other breeders. Why we did not put those two into the deep-freeze I cannot remember – perhaps we funked it. By that time Shadow's twin horns were already starting to curve back and down behind his ears. He was a tough, good-looking little ram and he was lent to a breeder with a small stock of experienced ewes for the first part of the covering season.

Biologically, sheep are very close to deer and with a breed like Jacobs, which is still very near to the wild, there is a distinct rut. From about the beginning of September the rams' necks thicken noticeably and they become possessive and aggressive, keeping close order with the ewes. Except in the case of knowledgeable old rams, they are continually sniffing up behind the ewes to see if they are in an interesting condition. When a ewe comes into season she is pestered until she yields and stands for the ram, usually letting him know she is ready, first by widdling and then by waggling her tail to the side. Before he mounts the ewe, the ram will often display, stretching his head to the sky with a curiously wrinkled nose and sneering lip. I have seen nearly identical displays by goats, and oddly enough, by stallions. The actual union always strikes me as unemotionally clinical and short, consisting of a few exploratory prods and one powerful surge. The ram may cover the ewe several times during her season.

Shadow came home from his autumn holiday obviously wiser but very glad to see us. One disadvantage of being on good terms with a large male animal is that, as they grow older, they can switch from playfulness to combative aggression very quickly. Shadow was no exception, and already in his first winter he developed the nasty habit of stalking you and either trying to bring you down with a quick butt at the back of the knees or hooking at your calves with a twist of his horns. If you turned on Shadow, he would back away with lowered head then come up behind you with a quick short stepping run as soon as you started walking again. He could be very persistent and one afternoon, when I was repairing fencing, I had to give him a full swung clout with a chestnut stake smack on his nose to make him stop.

Shadow's horns and his devotion to Sue cost us a gate. Soon after his return from learning stud work, Sue was talking to a colt in a field on the other side of the cart track which runs past the paddock. Shadow could hear Sue, but that was not good enough. He was bored and wanted to see her too. It was only the solid oak paddock gate which stopped him. A passerby who was watching told us afterwards that it took Shadow less than a minute, with stiff-necked shattering butts, to reduce that gate to matchwood. Having done so he simply stayed quite still in the paddock watching Sue through the gaping hole he had made for himself. Orion would have been a mile away in a trice.

# 6

# Big and Little

We have had dogs continuously in the family for years. The first of the run was a broken-coated black and white hunt terrier named Hi-Tickle. His sister, a smooth-coated little beauty we coveted but could not afford, was named Hi-Tum. Hi-Tickle – Tickle for short – was a character. He arrived as a present for Mark from my sister-in-law on Mark's sixth birthday. He was ideal for a small boy – an affectionate bundle of wiggle, lick and widdle. At that time we lived in the house in real commuter land, perched on the side of a steep slope, with long flights of steps running up to the back and front doors. A fairly busy road swept in a curve past the front gate, which was kept tight shut. We gave up trying to keep cats there. It was too heartbreaking.

Those steps were steep for a small pup and we could not help chuckling as he scrambled up them after Mark, every now and then giving his jaw a great crack as his front paws slipped from the top of the next step he had to negotiate. The flight of steps leading down and away from the back door was particularly steep. At the top of them was a small bush that Tickle spent his pennies by as soon as he learnt to ask to be let out. One evening it was I who answered his frantic calls and opened the door for him. I watched him as he trotted jauntily – looking very grown up – over to the bush. Instead of producing his usual puppy squat, he balanced on three legs, cocked the fourth leg behind him and looked up at me. He was plainly saying 'See what I can do.' Unfortunately, before he could celebrate his triumph, he overbalanced, fell down the top step and with indignant squeaks and yelps bounced all the way down to the bottom. I laughed until my sides ached. I still laugh to think of it – poor little devil – what a way to learn about pride coming before a fall.

We kept Tickle entire and, as he grew up, he took a keen interest in sex and developed the best nose for a bitch on heat I have ever known. How he got out we never knew, but he was always turning up, locked in the combat of canine love, up to three miles from home. We told our neighbours he had made himself a set of miniature step ladders, and grinned at the thought of him trotting up to the gate with the steps under his arm, when his nose told him it was time to get going. One time he went lost for two days and, eventually, fearing the worst, Ann telephoned the police. 'One foot high and snappy?' the policewoman on duty asked. 'That's him!' said Ann with feeling. He had bitten a policeman for interfering with his love life. But he got away with it and was let off with a caution.

He moved house with the rest of us, but soon started the dangerous game of running down the inside of the chain-link fence beside our drive, making mock attacks at the back wheels of the car. One morning he did it once too often – he was the wrong side of the fence and the back of the car swung in a rut. He must have slipped through the gate behind me without my knowledge. Poor Tickle.

We had always wanted a really big dog. The month after we moved I was introduced one evening to a long white furry caterpillar. Obviously missing its brothers and sisters, it was the picture of abject misery hiding behind very large paws. It was a bitch Pyrenean Mountain dog and we named her Fleur. The Forsyte *Saga* was the current television serial.

Pyreneans start slowly, but between about six weeks and six months they grow at a prodigious rate. Their food consumption during this period is important and enormous. To weigh Fleur I used to pick her up and get on the bathroom scales with her. I gave it up when she clocked nine stone. We calculated that in her prime she went to about twelve stone. In the Pyrenees they still grow them to fifteen stone.

Once she stopped growing, Fleur was a fussy and small eater. Pyreneans have a double coat; a heavy coarse white outer coat covering a thick lower layer of fine white wool – you can spin their combings incidentally – and this double insulation, coupled with a low metabolic rate, keeps their calorie requirement down. Fleur's favourite food when she grew up was eggs. From the time we had hens, any egg laid absentmindedly on the path by the house was neatly cracked open and licked out clean.

The first spring we had Fleur I left cutting the lawn until April. The grass was heavily infested with a thread-like speedwell – a beautiful invasive creeping weed originating in the Eastern Mediterranean. The speedwell produced a week of bloom which turned the whole lawn into a lake of milky blue. We captured a most lovely photograph of our young Pyrenean bitch lying, creamy white with black nose and lips and deep brown almond-shaped eyes, in that enormous haze of blue.

The garden is ideal for a Pyrenean. The terraces provided ledges on which Fleur could lie for hours – body stretched out, looking noble with her domed head held up and gazing out and away over the weald. In the heat of summer there is plenty of shade and there is also plenty of interesting water down by our spring system. Pyreneans love water – they are related to Newfoundlands – and at one time we nicknamed Fleur 'Bog Dog' for the number of times she appeared, coated in black wet smelly mud, happily expecting to be patted and played with.

The garden also has plenty of good burying spots. Fleur soon developed a liking for burying things. When we gave her bones she used to bury them, digging them up every few weeks and finding a new hiding spot. Once she swiped the Sunday joint and buried that. We found it in time though. Then she took to burying vegetables. One autumn I planted up a bed of desirable plants. Each plant was marked with a bamboo cane cut from the thicket by the spring. I cursed when March came round and nothing appeared. I cursed even more when, in April, potato shoots appeared by every stick. Fleur had dug up the lot and replaced them with potatoes! I found the plants eventually, all in a heap some yards away in the bushes with their naked roots licked lovingly clean. Fleur's best burying discovery was cauliflowers. She found out what only a dog could find out. A large cauliflower buried in early spring can be guaranteed, by early summer, to have acquired the rich ripe smell of very bad meat, just right for being dug up again. After some bad experiences we learnt to keep Fleur away from cauliflowers.

Pyreneans are sheep dogs, designed to protect flocks from very large predators. Although I suppose Fleur is many generations removed from a working strain, she still retains a herding instinct. When she was about a year old, she really got us worried. Tony put a flock of ewes in his field near our west boundary. Fleur is so large that it would need a six-foot fence to keep her in if she was really determined to get out. Fleur studied the flock carefully for a few minutes, then she was up, over and away, running in large circles round the sheep at high speed with her tail curled in a great cartwheel over her back. A twelve-stone Pyrenean Mountain dog at full pelt is quite a sight, but we could not stop to admire her. We had to get her out. We did, but half an hour later she was back in again. We had no alternative but to chain her up and tell Tony what had happened. Diana and Fleur were particular friends. Diana rode quietly and elegantly on her Arab gelding past our west boundary each morning: Fleur never failed to greet her with great woofs and tailwags. Tony agreed that it would be a shame to keep Fleur chained up, if it could be avoided. For a big powerful dog there had to be a big powerful cure for sheep chasing. There was. Fleur was locked for an afternoon in a stable with three rams. When we went to collect her, she was sitting exhausted on her haunches backed up against one wall. The three rams, equally exhausted, were on their haunches against the opposite wall. They only had strength left to look and glare across the stable at one another. It worked. Fleur gave sheep a wide berth from then on.

Fleur was devoted to Tickle and nothing pleased her so much as to take Tickle for a walk on a lead. The pair used to beetle off towards the woods, Fleur carrying the lead in her mouth with Tickle trotting obediently alongside. The real entertainment was to watch them sort themselves out after they had gone either side of a bush. Tickle would stand still, waiting patiently, one forepaw held off the ground, while his big friend puzzled the situation out. After Tickle died we waited two years before we replaced him with an almost identical hunt terrier bitch called Ticehurst. Her nickname was Tippy. When she arrived her length was about half of that of Fleur's head. We watched with some anxiety as Fleur approached the minute white newcomer sitting up in a basket. A small pink tongue curled out and licked the huge black nose. Everything was all right.

Tippy is Mark's dog and from an early age there was nothing she liked better than to go shooting with him. She soon found out all about rabbits and in contrast to Mark's relaxed walk, skittered through the undergrowth and bramble thickets ahead of him turning rabbits out. She would go on all day and come back with her coat full of thorns and her eyes bunged up from scratches. She learnt to settle herself down beside Mark's chair in the evening and wait for him to de-thorn her. They soon became an excellent combination.

Before Fleur became so stiff in her joints that we had to imprison her in the boiler room at night for her own good, she stayed outside in all weathers. Tippy has always been turned out at night unless Mark is home when, whatever is said, it is odds on that she will end up on Mark's bed, somewhere down by his feet. What Tippy liked best of all was to go dustbin raiding with Fleur.

If the weather was right, Fleur and Tippy would go out on their night patrol. Fleur simply jumped the fence. Tippy learned to climb it – or so I believe. C-J had a theory that Fleur lifted her over. Their raiding territory lay roughly within a two-mile radius of the house. That was just as well. A mile or so farther to the east and they would have been into woodland on the ridge protected by a gamekeeper who lays poisoned baits for foxes. If dogs are the victims – well, so far as that gamekeeper is concerned, it is the owner's fault for letting them wander. The technique they had devised was simple, but devastating. Fleur would push the dustbin over, knocking off the lid. Tippy would dart in, scratching the contents out with all four feet. The two of them would then pick the rubbish over and anything really smelly was selected to be brought home. There was never any doubt who the culprits were. Their ambitions were greater than their carrying capacity and they left a trail of odds and ends, usually wrapping paper, all the way through the woods to the spot in the fence where they got back in. Sometimes Tippy could not manage the climb back and we would find her next morning, all innocent on the doormat, when we took the milk in. On a really good night they did not content themselves with one dustbin. They would work their territory until daybreak and spend the next day exhausted, sleeping it off. Fleur's burying abilities really came into their own and after a major expedition I would be removing her treasures from the flower beds for weeks. There was an unspoken pact of silence with most of our neighbours on the subject, although they all knew perfectly well what was going on.

Quite often I come home from the office late at night. Every now and then as I turned into the cart track leading up to our drive, my headlights would pick out two white figures with black noses, half-concealed in the bushes by the side. They usually waited until I stopped beside them, opened the door and asked 'What have you two been doing then?' They would reply with a guilty wag of their tails and trot off into the night. Two white figures – Fleur, large and majestic – Tippy bouncing up and down, hock high beside her. It was a comical and heartwarming sight. Always the same words came to my mind – Big and Little.

# 7

# Great Balls of Fire

We were going to need more space. All the land we had
that was usable – and that was not much – was in use.
We only had the paddock at the bottom and some flat
land – just a few square yards – near the sheds at the top.
We had won ourselves a small rectangular vegetable
garden by filling in, and sculpting with a hired excavator,
a large hole left when ragstone had been quarried off the
site to build the house. The Frog was in use and there were
ramshackle chicken houses tucked into odd corners all
over the place. The small oblong stretch of grass below
the house was kept as a lawn as far as possible, but it was
usually occupied. Orphan lambs being reared for Tony
were tethered on it in spring. It was also used for putting

exercise runs down for small creatures needing air, grass and sunlight. At daybreak in the summer those runs became the focus of 'the stroll of the strumpets'. Large, fat woodpigeons, attracted by spilt food, waddled around, like so many plump, painted, be-ringed tarts, attended by their pimps – sleek, smooth-coated starlings who ducked and bobbed busying along on yellow feet keeping a professional eye open for likely customers. One year the run of a very ancient guinea-pig, called Spider, was moved round the lawn to different spots all summer. There must have been something special about Spider's droppings. In the autumn, wherever his run had been, the fungus threads running through the turf were excited into pushing up a nice fruiting crop of field mushrooms. We belive that Spider was the world's first dual-purpose guinea-pig.

Life as I saw it from the office became increasingly depressing. The social horizon was lit up by the flashes of deep-rooted industrial unrest, and lowering economic clouds muttered the threat of roaring inflation to come. We were enjoying ourselves, but we thought it wise to build into our activities some preparation for the worst. At the back of our minds was the philosophy of the old lady who curtsied in church each time the devil's name was mentioned – 'politeness costs nothing – and you never know !'

The sheds, all the chicken houses and a quite extraordinary garage – a mass of cracked asbestos sheets and woodworm infested timbers stuck together by the glue of decay – would have to go and be replaced by modern timber buildings. We made a three phase building plan. Phase one was to cover the erection of a long building consisting of a stable and a general-purpose barn – making a building twelve foot by forty foot overall – running along the north side of the vegetable garden. Two large new chicken houses, with fox-proof runs, would be put up along the south side. In phase two we would replace the garage with another general-purpose wooden building, of the same overall dimensions, in two sections each with separate access. We would also put up a general-purpose barn, twelve foot by thirty, at the east end of the vegetable garden. Phase three would consist of the addition of lean-tos of various kinds to the new buildings. We believed that in three years' time, if only we could rent some more land, we would be well placed to fend for ourselves to a considerable degree.

Planning is one thing, execution is quite another. Phase one involved pulling down the existing sheds and that meant finding new homes for the inhabitants. The shed population had fluctuated, but there was still rather a lot of it. We had lost our tame tawny owl, named Minerva and reared from a chick, some time back with aspergillosis, a fungus disease which attacks the lungs of any creature, but to which birds are particularly prone. She had shared one end of a shed with Snapdragon and Co. – the game bantams crossed Andalusian. She roosted above the nesting boxes and at feeding time would fly freely to take meat, plastered with rabbit fur to aid her digestion – if owls don't regurgitate pellets of fur, chitin and bone they die – from a gloved fist. She would return with it to her perch and tear at it with ferocious delicacy, looking piercingly up and across to us from time to time. She was more interesting than lovable. She never lost her wild pride, although we could not persuade her to leave us and fend for herself – she simply did not know how to. When the fungus struck she had gone in a matter of days. Mark was very upset when Minerva died. Julia heard of this and sent him up a charming little sketch in pen and colour wash of a young tawny owl. This act of kindness was typical of Julia. Her knowledge of local affairs stemmed partly from sharp ears on lending-library nights and partly from a willingness to listen sympathetically at other times. A bit incoherent when it came to words, she had the knack of giving – a sketch, some eggs and suchlike – at just the moment when help was needed most. Much better than words, those little gifts told people they were thought of.

Snapdragon and Co. were turfed out into one of the antique chicken houses which was patched up for them. Bagpipes and his mongrel wives ran free in the rest of that shed. They were rounded up and put into another antique. Bagpipes made such a fuss that we had to let him out again. For the next three years he became a sort of unpaid foreman, stalking inquisitively about, keeping a shiny eye on proceedings.

The next shed was occupied entirely by Tippets and his wives. Tippets was a cock Golden pheasant. His hens were as meek, brown and dowdy as he was multi-coloured and gorgeous. The breed takes its name from the golden cresting of the cock bird. He took his name from his orange and black neck hackles which are known to tiers of sea-trout flies as tippets. They are shy birds and you can only breed from them in captivity if they have plenty of room and a large dark airy space with plenty of shrubs, stems and other cover into which the hens can retreat to build their nests – basically a scrape on the ground – and to brood their eggs and young. This kind of facility was easily made. The back of the shed was falling away and a bamboo thicket was invading it. We had simply given the back an encouraging push, cut some additional bamboo to thicken up the cover and encased the whole artificial thicket with old sacking and chicken wire. Tippets and his wives did their stuff and Sue had a nice sideline selling off young Golden pheasants to other would-be breeders. The eggs are a dull pale olive and they in turn provide a remarkable contrast to the strutting cock bird. The chicks are like all game bird chicks. Round, downy and active from birth with mottled camouflage markings and the ability to freeze at the command of their watchful mother.

We decided to let Tippets and his wives go wild in the

garden knowing that in time they would find their way over the fence and into the woods. There are plenty of pheasants round us and relatively little shooting. Part of the land is owned by the National Trust. They hung around the garden for a few days and then melted quietly away. We thought they would manage for themselves all right. The only alternative would have been the Frog, and we doubted if they were robust enough to stand up to bullying by the guinea-fowl.

We kept a trio of guinea-fowl, a cock and two hens on the Frog. They had been bought as dual-purpose, but although they were ornamental in a hideous way, with their horned vulturine heads, and set up a great scolding and cackling at the approach of anyone or anything, they were useless as providers of eggs or meat. Each year the hens would conceal huge clutches of eggs – sometimes in separate nests, sometimes in a communal nest like a large double bed. We never found those eggs until the birds were sitting on them. Each year the cock bird would kill off the chicks as they hatched. He was quite horrible about it and would not leave the little corpses alone until he had torn the heads off. We consulted other breeders and they could only suggest removing the cock bird as soon as the hens were sitting. It was not a good suggestion. We could not catch him by day, and by night he roosted high up in a holly tree which grows, in company with beech, birch and fir, on the Frog.

One year a Silky went broody at the right time and we popped some guinea-fowl eggs under the white, downy, blue wattled and wingless hen. Silkies are devoted foster-mothers and when some half dozen eggs hatched we thought we could really look forward to roast guinea-fowl in the autumn. It was a wet year and, despite all the Silky's devotion, they only survived a few weeks. Guinea-fowl are excellent watch dogs and some of their feathers are useful for fishermen, but, in our experience, they are unreliable for anything else. Perhaps the Frog confined them too closely.

After the animals had been removed, the usable contents of the shed were arranged in a sort of gypsy encampment under the nearby beech trees. Then came the main demolition work. Some of the corrugated iron from the roof came off complete and was good enough to make the sides of a compost heap for a year or two. In the case of most of it, at the first screech of protest as I pulled the old drive nails through the ridges, the metal tore along the gulleys like dry tissue and crumbled entirely away. Years of leaves rotting as they lay in the autumn had rusted it through. It was great fun bringing the frames of the first two sheds down. I simply tied a long rope to one corner and rocked the building. There is something very satisfying in permissible destruction and the more cataclysmic the final induced collapse, the better. The death rattle of those sheds gave me a warm feeling of safety and guilt mixed together.

The remaining shed had originally housed the petrol driven generator which provided the house with its first electricity. It had also powered the pump to lift water from the top of the spring system, which emerged halfway down one side of the garden at the junction of clay and greensand, to large storage tanks in the roof. The generator had gone long since and only the concrete bed was left. A pair of swallows stuck their mud nest each year on the rafters above the generator bed and in summer we admired them as they swooped low, twittering with anger, and 'dive bombed' the cat, buffeting her head with their wings, if she came too near the shed.

That third shed was not going to succumb to a pull on a rope. It was stoutly built and the chamber which had housed the generating plant was walled with close boards, lined with asbestos cladding on the inside and covered with tarred felt on the outside. I had a large pile of re-usable timber from the first two sheds stacked away in my encampment under the beech trees, so I thought I would give the family a treat. I announced a bonfire spectacular that night. 'What about the asbestos?' Ann asked. 'Oh – that will just crumble away into a sort of white powder,' I replied. 'Stupid question,' I thought. With everyone assembled, I put a match to a dead ivy stump on the windward side of the shed. For a while it went as expected. Tongues of deep red flame sprang through the top, licking up through the clouds of black smoke released as the tarred felt caught up. Then a whole series of sharp bangs started. 'Godfathers!' said Ann. Startled out of my self-satisfaction, I could only think that an old box of cartridges had been hidden away and was going up. I moved the family quickly to a safe distance and looked back to the dramatic eruption that was taking place. It was not cartridges, it was the asbestos cladding exploding. As it exploded, it sent large fragments, with flaming wood and tarred felt attached, soaring high into the air. Suddenly it came to me – 'Great balls of fire!' Ann and I come from the generation who had their tails set alight by Elvis Presley and Jerry Lee Lewis. Perhaps this was a symbolic welcome as we fell back through time into a second childhood. The show must have been seen and heard down in the village. C-J told us later that various descriptions of it turned up in the free compositions submitted by her fellow pupils to Miss Fitch. C-J was rising eleven and in the middle of her last term at the village school. Miss Fitch had given C-J a jolly good start. The results of her discipline were all right by us.

The next day the garden looked as if it were covered by a multitude of miniature Red Indian camps as small piles of wood and felt sent their smoke signals spiralling into the still morning air. It was strangely beautiful. The dogs were very impressed. They stood on the tarmac path above the lawn and looked around and down. Tippy, the hunt terrier, who had a litter of pups upstairs by Sue's bed at the time – lifted her head and started to howl. Fleur, with her huge, wolf-like howl, joined in. Those two idiots singing away into the silence, with the smoke wreaths rising and the woods and cliff looking quietly on, completed the air of unreality which marked the beginning of phase one. I was all too conscious that with the sheds down, ramshackle though they had been, we had burnt our boats behind us.

# 8

# Twist and Shout

We were in deep trouble. Or rather, I was in deep trouble. Ann and the two girls had an unmistakable 'You got us into this, you can get us out again' expression on their faces.

The day after we had set fire to the last shed, I raked the site clean. It looked neat and tidy and flat, save for the old generator bed. I thought it should not take long to break that up with a sledge hammer. The fragments would come in handy as hardcore for the foundations of the new building and the stable floor. It took a morning, but at the end of it the pyramidical lump of concrete was scattered strategically all over the site. I stepped back a few paces to admire my handiwork. Something was wrong. The site was still neat and tidy, but it did not look flat any more. With the emphasis of the generator bed at one end gone, the site had taken a nasty downward lurch at one corner. It had looked flat enough while the sheds were there. The rather quaint way in which they had sprawled about the place – and which we had liked so much – became uncomfortably significant. I comforted myself with the thought that it might be in my imagination and went off to lunch. A nasty empty feeling was spreading inside me which lunch did nothing to fill. On the contrary, lunch coalesced into a hard tight knot while the emptiness spread and swirled liquidly about it.

We had decided to buy a well-known make of prefabricated building. The manufacturers left one in no doubt that they wanted nothing to do with the construction of a base – they would provide detailed drawings though – and that they were not too keen on being involved in erection. The invitation to share the view that their part in the affair should stop at their factory gate was clear. It seemed fair enough to me. I had ordered our building – it consisted of two of their standard units put together – and asked for drawings of a base the building would fit. The drawings had arrived the previous day. The pleasure I was getting out of licensed destruction and anticipation of the fiery fun to come had quelled the slight uneasiness I felt on noticing that strict compliance with the drawings would require me to be accurate to within five millimetres.

I was beginning to realize what I had taken on. Those excellent buildings were probably at least batch produced, if not mass produced, and could well be made to tolerances of five millimetres if the timber was seasoned. The building was to stand on a raised brick base. I had never laid a brick in my life, but it had seemed to me that two courses of bricks, laid in a simple rectangle, with gaps for a door and a barn entrance, should not be too difficult, given time

68

and patience. But five millimetres is less than the bulge on an awkward brick and the complication, if the site really did sag at one end, was quite alarming. I had never set out foundations before either. And each time I had done it in my head I had started with nice level ground.

After lunch I surveyed the sight with the help of Sue and C-J. Our equipment consisted of straight iron bars of equal length – the sort for making upper windows infant proof – a big ball of white string, a sixty-foot tape measure and a nine-inch spirit level. Setting out the pins on the assumption that the site was flat was simple. I knocked up a big three-four-five triangle to give me right-angled corners and measured the diagonals of the site using Pythagoras.

Having got the iron bars driven in upright to the same depth and in the right places, we started the survey. The technique was simple. I chose the corner with the most comfortable bit of ground to lie on, and tied the end of the string twelve inches down from the top of the bar marking the corner. C-J then ran the string to the bar at the next corner, held it twelve inches down and pulled it tight so that it pressed against the intermediate marking bars. I squinted down the line to be sure that it was taut and straight and delicately balanced the spirit level on the string at my end. Sue, standing above me, told me where the bubble was. On the two sides running at right angles from that first corner, it worked like a dream. So far as we could make out, the site was dead level along those lines of survey. Thoughts of boasting at the office of accuracies of even one millimetre started to prick and fizz like champagne in my mind.

After the intoxication came the hangover. The crucial side – the one with the stable door and the huge gap for the barn entrance – rippled like a switchback and plunged out of sight at the far end. The bars only protruded eighteen inches above the ground. We had to lash two together to prove that the site dropped about two feet along that line of forty feet. I was so unnerved that I made the girls measure it with me again and again to confirm the awful fact. Although it was midsummer, it was nearly dark before we finished. The girls were tired and fed up and in my head that wretched five millimetres expanded, contracted and twanged like an india rubber band.

The next day was Saturday and the family gave me a wide berth. Even the cat kept out of the way. In the middle of the morning Providence smiled on us and sent a shaft of sunlight to cheer things up. The sunlight went by the name of Len and he arrived with the weekend joint. Len was the butcher's roundsman – a large, bald headed, cheerful man in his sixties who had done a great many things in his life. I knew that amongst other things he had been a master cooper. The staves of barrels have to be cut with great accuracy, certainly within tolerances of five millimetres. Len looked the sort of man who had a reassuring fund of general practical knowledge. I asked him if he would be so kind as to inspect the site with me.

Len confirmed the obvious. There was a choice of either doing a lot of digging or of building up the base wall to the correct level from the lowest point. In fact there was no choice. Whilst driving home the iron bars we had found that about a foot below ground level, was a bed of solid ragstone. Len did point out that a lot of work would be saved by stepping the foundations. Len had strained himself trussing turkeys the previous Christmas, he could offer me token assistance laying bricks and nothing more. If I wanted advice that was another matter. Len became my technical consultant and at the weekends, seated on a chair in the sun, with his tummy on his knees, a pint in his hand and a cheerful smile on his great round face he set about educating me. Even Bagpipes entered into the spirit of the thing and ignored the challenge of Len's legs.

Luck was with us. The weather stayed fine at the weekends. Len was a firm but cheerful task master. He knew a great deal. The footings were dug, mainly by Mark who hated the job, and passed by a scrupulously polite young building inspector. The foundations were laid and passed as well, complete with their steps, carefully measured out with the proper allowance for the bricks and mortar to come. I calculated afterwards that the stable flooring and the foundations took four tons of concrete in its wet state. I had knocked this up, carted it, and laid it by hand at the rate of a ton a day. It cost me blistered hands, a sore back and a bent wheelbarrow. Then came the walling. Len had been a bit sniffy about my nine-inch spirit level and instructed me to buy a bigger one. He approved of my big three-four-five triangle though, and short of buying or borrowing some very expensive equipment, could not suggest an alternative to the ball of string technique for getting the levels right.

I started at the end which had to be built up. I soon found that laying bricks is not so easy. I was very slow and wasted large quantities of mortar because it had usually 'gone off' before I could get round to using it. I found that, even when I had mastered the general idea, there were nasty snags. The thing that really got me was the combined properties of bricks and water. If I kept the bricks dry, they sucked all the water out of the mortar as soon as they touched it, so that there was no time to wiggle the brick into its correct position. If I wetted the brick, the thing kept swimming about for the next half hour, so that I was continuously held up while I pushed bulges in the wall back into place. Len smiled happily into his pint and let me work out my own salvation. I think it was his revenge for my refusal to accept his advice and piddle in the mortar to keep it from 'going off'.

There was another difficulty with the bricks. I had dug up from time to time, from various parts of the garden, a large quantity of nice old bricks. I had stored these under cover to dry them out. I had hoped there would be enough of these to face the base wall and had bought an equal quantity of ordinary, sand faced, building bricks for the courses on the inside. It gradually dawned on me that the bricks were of differing lengths. We checked the whole lot. The old bricks were a uniform nine inches, with scarcely any deviation. Of the new bricks only about one fifth were the desired nine inches. The rest varied a full half-inch either side of this. Len said he believed this was due to mass production which allowed different rates of shrinkage while the bricks were in the kiln. He told me that when he was a boy, and before he was apprenticed to a master cooper, he had helped his father make building bricks by hand. They got one shilling a hundred for them and were glad of it. Their customers allowed them no deviation from standard size.

At last the walling was finished and it did not look too bad. According to the tape measure, the doorway, barn entrance and overall dimensions were within the magical five millimetres – more or less. Judging by the stretches of string, the top line had a few sags and humps on roller-coaster lines. I gladly took comfort in Len's remark that a wooden building 'likes to have the chance to settle down a bit'. We had plenty of time in hand for the walling to dry out before the building arrived in sections in early autumn.

Delivery day arrived. I had taken the day off from the office, and paced up and down waiting for the noise of a lorry. It came late in the afternoon. It was piled high with the most enormous building sections and was driven by a minute, skinny, sandy-haired little Scot. He enquired where the unloading gang was. I was half-way through explaining to an increasingly incredulous driver that the sections were to be unloaded by me, and him I hoped, when providential help arrived again. It was a removal van delivering an old upright piano that had been given to C-J by her godmother.

There were four brawny men with it and two heavy-duty trolleys. In no time the sections were off the lorry and stacked in a huge pile inside the back gate. The little Scot, who, despite his size had proved to have the strength of a Goliath, went on his way, scratching his head.

It was clear that I was going to need help getting the sections down to, and erected on, the site. I consulted Len again, borrowed a large four-wheeled barrow and persuaded two incautious friends to help for a day. With Len guiding and putting propping poles into the right place at the right time, it was surprisingly easy. By the end of the day we had the walls up and bolted together, the roof trusses in and two roof sections on. That was as far as the four of us could get. We had just managed the roof sections at the stable end, where the brick base was shallowest. We simply could not reach as the base grew deeper towards the other end, and the trusses soared away from our reach. The only solution was to take the remaining sections to pieces and reassemble them at roof level. This was something for me to get on with by myself. With parting advice from Len to remember how the sections had been put together, the three of them left me to it.

It was a long job. First I dismembered the sections completely, remembering Len's advice and using red crayon identification marks liberally. That took a week of evening work. Reassembly was organized with me up the ladder and one of the family passing timber up to me. The only snag was that, when the sections had been made, the boards had been cramped together. I could not reproduce that pressure. I kept on getting embarrassing half boards at the end of each section. In between sorting that out with a rip saw, the work developed a really lively rhythm of its own. I would nail home a board, turn and call to whoever was helping, and hold my hand down for them to put the next board into it. Up came the board, bang bang went the hammer and so on. Before long the roof assembly was going to the tune and beat of *Twist and Shout*. We all liked Beatle music and I enjoyed myself so much I nearly fell off the ladder.

Once the roof sections were on, that was really it. I spent a few happy evenings scampering about the roof in gym shoes putting the felt on and one day with a friend fixing a plastic guttering system. We were there. We had our first agricultural building up. Len had been right. The building quietly settled to the curves of the brick base. When I thought of the things that could have gone wrong without Providence producing Len and the chaps bringing C-J's piano, I sweated quietly.

The rest of phase one was started that winter. New chicken houses were an exorbitant price. So we bought two garden sheds in an end of season sale. I took them to pieces in the sitting-room while Ann was on holiday, and carted them off to be pressure-treated against rot. I put them together again in the sitting-room – Ann was back and resigned to the situation. I made alterations such as entry flaps for the birds as I went along.

One was up and in use by Christmas. It housed a dozen Cuckoo Maran hens who gave us lovely brown eggs that looked homely and cheerful at breakfast time. The other chicken house had to await the demise of Parsley. There were a number of Sue's old age pensioners about the place and Parsley was one of them. Actually, he had belonged originally to C-J, but Sue took him over. He was a large and very old white rabbit. It was understood in the family that old age pensioners were allowed to die in peace and dignity. Some of them held out for a long time. Spider – our dual-purpose guinea-pig, had been one of them. He seemed to go on forever with his teeth growing bigger and bigger. Finally Spider died in his sleep and Sue erected a plywood marker on his grave bearing the words 'Spider – Good Old Chap'. I said I liked the 'Good Old Chap' bit. Sue, embarrassed but honest, explained that it was a mistake

74

because it started as 'God Bless Him', but the spelling of God had gone wrong.

We had been able to move Spider around, but we could not move Parsley. His hutch would not stand a move and we didn't think that asking an old gentleman like him to change houses fitted in with the peace and dignity idea. Parsley moved on to his own other world in late winter. In the early spring of the year following the demolition of the old sheds, the second hen house and its adjoining run was occupied by a flock of pullets – Rhode Island crossed Light Sussex coming into their first lay. Phase one was complete.

# 9

# Angus and Ogilvy

The year after the new stable building went up, I spent the summer recapturing the garden. Since moving to the house we had put a lot of effort into the garden. The plan had been to contrive ways of growing interesting plants without disturbing the general wildness of the place. This had meant the creation of a large number of camouflaged island beds. I had little time for gardening whilst I was learning my bricklaying and weeds had sneaked in everywhere. The wet land by the spring system was worst. It had grown a lush jungle of bramble and mare's tail that sprawled everywhere. It was so thick and luxuriant that we always expected to find 'nasties' lying in wait to twine round our ankles as we forced a passage through.

On the animal front everything was going reasonably well. The autumn before we had crossed Shadow back to his mother Sixpence and she had produced nice twin ram lambs. Bramble and Tiger Lily had produced three ewe lambs between them – also sired by Shadow. But nine sheep in the paddock, even if five were suckling lambs, was pushing our luck. It was all right as long as the weather was showery and kept the grass growing. But if the weather was dry we had to feed them. This was expensive. We needed more land urgently.

There were plenty of odd fields about the place that people would make available for ponies. But sheep were a different matter. Orion was long gone but his escapades had not given our sheep a very good reputation. Sue searched the neighbourhood. She got a sympathetic hearing but nothing else. Then we had a stroke of luck. Q heard of Sue's search. Q and his family live in one of a group of houses tucked into the edge of the woods well back from the top of the ridge, and about a mile to the north-east of us. At one time Q had been with the Colonial Service in the Pacific. He had maintained a link with that part of the world by taking on the official representation in London of one of the phosphate rich islands which had regained its independence. He owned a six-acre field, with two dilapidated shelters, and a half acre of woodland to it, beside the road running up the ridge from the village and only ten minutes' walk from our house. The land was sick from too much grazing by horses without a rest, but the fencing was fairly sound.

Q and his wife Jill had learnt the value of land during their time abroad. They liked to see it used properly. Q wrote to Sue saying he had heard she was trying to expand our venture with animals, and that he rather approved of the idea. Sue read the letter wide-eyed. Q's proposal was that we should use the field for agricultural purposes

77

rent free, provided we spent a sum equal to its farm rental value each year on keeping it in proper order. It was an inspired and generous offer. It gave Sue great faith in mankind in general and Q in particular. It also broadened our horizons. We jumped at the offer in June, with a possibility of possession of the field in September.

Julia boomed words of approval and informed us that the field was very fertile and had produced good cereal crops in past years, before it had been allowed to revert to pasture. Horses are wasteful and selective feeders and the areas of fine grass in the field were heavily infested with weeds – particularly dock and creeping thistle. The uninfested areas carried coarse grass growing from a heavy thatch of old roots and stems. Friends of ours, who scratched a happy but precarious living from the sides of Dartmoor, told us the quickest and easiest way to get the land in order would be to graze it with sheep and bullocks, take a hay crop and graze it with bullocks again.

We had sheep, but we did not have bullocks. It was a year of crisis for beef farmers. Shortage had been followed by gross overproduction. Fat stock were being sold everywhere at a loss and calf prices were on the floor. Sue and Ann went to Haywards Heath market and came back with two, one-week-old, bull calves wrapped in sacking and laid out on either side of Sue on the back seat of our Mini. Sue had explained to the auctioneer that she wanted animals that would be suitable for beef and he had helped her pick those two out. One had cost eighteen pounds, the other sixteen. The auctioneer's assistant helped Sue and Ann remove the two babies from their pen and load them into the back of the car. Without really thinking about it we had acquired our first pure farm animals. Bullocks are kept for one purpose only, food.

One of the calves was jet black and already showing signs of becoming solid beef from his knees up. It seemed likely that his knees would never be far off the floor, however much he grew above them. We realized afterwards that he was bred from a Friesian cow by a Sussex bull. But at the time we thought he was an Aberdeen Angus, and Angus was what we called him. The other, a leggy, the big-framer roan, had to be called Ogilvy. We simply could not resist the temptation. A childish quirk I expect, but the idea appealed to the family sense of humour.

Angus and Ogilvy had to be bucket fed. They were installed in the stable with plenty of straw bought from Tony. Sue reared them with her usual maternal care and introduced C-J to the duties of first reserve. They were kept in the stable until they had recovered from the setback caused by castration and Sue had weaned them off the bucket on to hard food. They were a friendly pair. As soon as anyone appeared they came crowding to the stable door, ears pricked, eyes rolling and nostrils flared. They liked standing while their cold wet noses were stroked and they explored the wrists of the stroker with their wet rough tongues. Angus had a tongue of nice grey-blue colour, Ogilvy's tongue was pink and tan, like a hound's belly. Their only disagreeable habit was of standing nose to tail sucking at each other's navel. As a result they each developed a soggy flap of skin that hung down under them like a small pink envelope. We never cured them of the habit. Whether they did it because of boredom or because of a desire to suckle I don't know. I suppose it gave them the same sense of satisfaction that thumb-sucking gives a baby.

I thought they were at their nicest when their horn buds were just showing through. If you offered them the palm of your hand, they rubbed their faces against it, from the tips of their noses through to their ears and back again. I used to think of their small heads as 'nubbly'. It was the only word I could think of which described the sensation. They were at the stage when sturdy young bullocks were emerging from small affectionate calves.

When the calves were weaned off the bucket, they were turned out into the overcrowded paddock with the sheep. We had to supplement the very meagre diet of grass available with concentrates the whole time. They soon got used to living with sheep. We turned our attention to the approaching autumn and plans for Q's field.

We decided that, as soon as we obtained possession of the field, we would put the bullocks into it and then split it into two sections – one of four acres and the other of two acres. We planned to enclose the two-acre section in sheep netting to take the Jacobs. A small stream running down the west side of the field ensured there would be no water problems if we ran the dividing fence from east to west. This way, the smaller section would include a small wooden shelter which had been used at some time as a milking parlour. It needed some repair, but would be useful at lambing time. There would also be a tree-covered bank included, where the sheep could shelter from cold winds and the heat of summer. The bigger section would include a larger shelter which needed rebuilding – and a half acre of woodland, with a spring system bubbling up in it, which would provide an ample playground for cattle.

When we put the bullocks into the field, they looked ridiculously small and lost. No sooner were they in, than they galloped off, stiff tailed, to hide in the woodland. When they heard the sound of feed nuts rattling in the old zinc bath we had brought down for them, they galloped all the way back to us.

With plenty of grass, Angus and Ogilvy started to grow well and they liked nothing better than to career round and round us, snorting, kicking and tossing their growing horns as we worked in the field that winter. When Angus had a mind to, he could look black, mysterious and sinister. Ogilvy was just a great clown and never managed to look anything else.

Work on the field progressed well. We had decided to

invest in stout three-foot netting for the sheep section. We strung this round the outer perimeter first. There were plenty of good straining posts, made out of portions of telegraph pole, already in the outer fence. Once we had slashed back the heavy growth of sloe and bramble that was invading the field, the job was simple. Gate posts and straining posts were set in place along the dividing line over one weekend. Soft clay and a hole-borer like a giant gimlet made digging holes, three feet deep to take posts, a simple job. The rest of the division, with intermediate chestnut stakes, sheep netting and a topping of two strands of barbed-wire taking the fence up to four feet high, followed the next weekend.

With Angus and Ogilvy imprisoned in the large lower section, we were ready to put the small flock of the three ewes and three large ewe lambs in the top section. One of Sixpence's two ram lambs had been sold to another breeder. Shadow and the other were to spend the winter in the paddock. The ewes had not been caught all together since the days of the great escape. They had been caught individually to be shorn and wormed and have their feet trimmed. But collection as a flock was a distant and exciting memory.

Probably we should not have tried it, but, once we had started, the sheep entered into the spirit of the game with such enthusiasm that we had no choice but to go on. The sheep insisted on keeping together as a flock. It was now near midwinter and the animals were round, with heavy fleeces. One of the first things a Jacob sheep does when fresh and threatened with capture is to start bouncing, stiff-legged with a bowed back, straight up into the air. The habit probably comes from their wild origin when, like some of the antelope species, they jumped high, in order to get a better view, both of approaching danger and the best way of escape. We were not inclined to encourage this bouncing anywhere near the paddock fence. With the flock clustered in the centre, looking at us high-headed and suspicious, Sue and I had a tactical conference. Memories of earlier experiences flooded back. A bucket of nuts and a herring net! Sue brought a bucket half filled with pony nuts and rattled it. I stood stock still beside her with a folded portion of herring net hidden behind my back. Greed soon overcame suspicion and, when the flock gathered round, pushing at each other to get at the nuts Sue had spilt on the ground, I quietly draped the net over them. Their horns protruded through the netting and fixed them. We held our breath. To our enormous relief they stood docile, waiting quite placidly while we hauled them out from under the netting one by one – put head collars on them and tied them to the paddock rails. There the ewes waited their turn to be led to the trailer standing up the cart track. Once let loose in their new field, they made a beeline for the tree-covered slope. From under the trees they turned and peered back at us with wild black and yellow eyes, while Angus and Ogilvy rocketed back and forth on their side of the dividing fence complaining with loud bellows because their old friends would not come down and play with them.

When March came round, the two bullocks were put into the sheep section so that the four acres could have a chance to produce our first hay crop. It was lambing time. Angus and Ogilvy went through an unhappy six weeks whilst Shadow, who had rejoined the flock, smashed into their legs full tilt if they came too near. They would lumber away shaking a bruised shin with a hurt look on their faces. They never could understand why suddenly they were so unwelcome. Once the lambs were really strong, the problem was over and they grazed along quite happily with the flock while Shadow went into his summer solitary retreat. He grazed quietly in his own corner of the field, waiting for the covering season to start again.

We had a wonderful hay crop that year. I had borrowed a spinner in the March, hitched it to the back of the Land-Rover – we had graduated from the Mini by then – and spread nitro-chalk pellets to fertilize the field. That grass had not been allowed to grow to seed for years and, given a good send-off by the nitrogen, it soon went to a dark green three feet. The thistles and the docks went with it. Our first hay crop was nourishing but prickly.

We cut and baled the hay with the help of a contractor – four hundred and twenty bales of it – three weeks before erection of the hay barn up at the house, under phase two of the building programme, was due. So, temporarily, it had to go into a stack on the field with a black plastic sheet over it to keep the weather off. We were running short of keep in the sheep section, but we did not dare open up the whole field whilst our precious stack of hay was there. Each evening I used to inspect the stack on my way home from the office to make sure it was not heating up. The bales had been dampened by a slight rainfall while we were collecting them up and we were worried by the possibility of a rick fire. There was never any heating up, but there were soon tell-tale pats of dung in the vicinity of the stack. I inspected the dividing fence to see where the bullocks were getting through, but there was no break anywhere. The mystery was soon solved. Ogilvy had learned to jump. I saw him do it one evening. He wandered casually up to the fence, sat back on his hocks and propelled himself over the fence with an ungainly bunny hop. Once over, he trotted gaily over to the stack and loosened wisps from a corner bale with his curling horns. Angus stayed on his side of the fence, bellowing his impotent annoyance. He was so beefy and short in the leg he stood no chance of following Ogilvy over. He would bucket along the fence with his great big black barrel of a belly swaying from side to side. But jumping was out.

With the stack carted up to the house, the whole field was opened up to the sheep and the bullocks. Angus and

Ogilvy had until the autumn to put on the weight we wanted to see. They did their best and ate their heads off. The floor of the half acre of woodland grew a lush green grass which they adored and the spring system provided them with a cool, black, mud wallow when they wanted to relax. By the October they were sixteen months old and had grown to a respectable seven hundredweight each. They were small as bullocks go, but if we ran them on through the winter, living out in the open, we would have to feed them concentrates to keep their weight and condition.

## 10

# White Rocks Splashdown

If you rear calves, which you know by name, by hand, you are likely to get fond of them. That is what happened to Sue with Angus and Ogilvy. Mixing the dried milk substitute with warm water in the kitchen and taking the buckets up to the bawling babies in the stable soon became a labour of love. It was an understandable, but unwelcome development. The significance of the step we had taken from the dual-purpose idea was dawning on all of us.

After about a week of it, Sue came up with a suggestion of her own. She told me that, whilst she realized perfectly well that the two bullocks were to be killed for meat eventually, it would be easier to put that out of her mind, while she was feeding them, if she also had something to feed which she could keep. I asked her what was in her mind. 'A baby Jersey,' she replied. 'If we can find a heifer calf, we can have her as a house-cow and share her milk with her calf when she has one.' It was a seductive idea and any twinge of doubt I had was dispelled by the thought that, if we found a heifer calf when the two bullocks were weaned, it would be a long time before she had calved and was a milk producer. It was probable that we would have a milk surplus, but perhaps we could use that on pigs. I kept quiet about that idea. I did not want to add to our commitments and the second phase of the building programme was not yet started.

Sue and I set off in the Mini one Saturday in August to find a Jersey heifer. Our plan was simple. We would drive quietly into Sussex, keeping to the main road, until we found a farm advertising its ownership of a pedigree Jersey herd. We knew there were plenty about and sooner or later we were bound to find one which was prepared to sell a baby heifer.

We were lucky with our second herd. The farmer's wife directed us to her husband, who was helping out with his tractor at a local gymkhana. He sent us back to his wife, with good wishes and permission to take one of three heifers he had, under a week old, in exchange for five pounds. It seemed too good to be true. We knew that male Jersey calves usually went for one pound to the pet food factories, but a pedigree Jersey heifer for five pounds – that really was something. The afternoon took on a holiday atmosphere.

The farmer's wife was charming. She showed us the three calves, but would not let us choose until she had shown us their mothers. It was milking time and the herd was queuing up in an orderly fashion to go into the milking parlour. Each cow wore a large green plastic collar bearing an identification number. One of the mothers was a really big beast with large gentle eyes and a lovely colour. She was one of those Jerseys with her back, flank and head a dark bay and with a rich cream colour covering her under-parts. We chose her calf. All Jersey calves are particularly beautiful and, with their enormous eyelashes, are much nearer to deer in their appearance than cattle.

The calf was wrapped in a sack and cuddled on Sue's lap in the back of the car. I parted with a five pound note and we started home. I drove slowly. It was a lovely after-noon and we felt we had done well. After a while we started to discuss a possible name. The sight of those cows had fired our imaginations. We had no doubt that the calf was to be part of the foundation stock of a famous pedi-gree herd. We both had visions of some future sale ring and a great auctioneering firm telling an impressed ring of anxious buyers 'And here gentlemen are the lots you have been waiting for. A few fine heifers from off the ridge. You know what that means gentlemen – an un-usual opportunity, so don't let's waste each other's time. Who'll start me at a thousand guineas for this little beauty?' It was entrancing nonsense but it did concentrate our minds on the necessity of a herd-name. That auctioneer of the future was not going to get very far without a herd-name – and an impressive one at that.

We decided fairly quickly on White Rocks. There is a vertical cliff of pure ragstone near our house which carried that name on maps right back into the eighteenth century. It was a good name for Jerseys and went well with Way-ward – the flock-name of the Jacob sheep. The second name proved more difficult. The calf looked so innocent and fawnlike and all the names that came naturally to our minds were already the copyright of Walt Disney. 'Let's think about it when we get home,' Sue suggested. 'Good idea,' I said. The calf had other ideas. A long liquid noise settled the matter decisively – Splashdown ! The poor little brute had decided not to hold on any more and had let everything go.

I drove on rather more quickly after that. The lovely afternoon was also rather warm and the liquid dung of a bucket-reared calf has a more pungent odour than that of a grass-fed cow. Sue was not at all amused, and not only because of the state of her legs. She thought that the name Splashdown – although apt and justified – smacked too much of the exercise of my slightly malicious humour at the expense of one of her babies. 'You call her Splash and I'll call her Paddy,' was her suggestion. It seemed most illogical, but Sue never offered an explanation and I did not press her for one. I knew better. We disagreed peacefully on the subject and the rest of the family soon got used to the idea that what was Paddy to Sue was Splashdown to me. Sue eventually added to the name confusion – out of sheer cussedness I suspect – and back-tracked to Patrick, mainly on the grounds that Paddy was the diminutive applicable to babies and the baby was growing up. She remained Splashdown to me, although I soon fell into the habit of using the shorter form – Splash.

Mark and I went on a fishing holiday soon after the arrival of Splashdown. We rented a small stone cottage up in the north-east of Scotland. We had two miles of fishing on a dramatic little river that sings down through deep gorges cut over thousands of years by great granite boulders swept down off the hills and grinding a bed through the soft sandstone in the lower reaches. If there is much water in that river, the song turns into a snarl and in a real spate the snarl becomes a sullen heavy roar.

In August that fishing costs next to nothing. The nets are still on the estuary and very few salmon have arrived off the coast by that time after travelling from their distant feeding grounds. Nevertheless it was bliss. There were shoals of small sea-trout moving to the fly at night and a few brown trout of about half a pound which could be wheedled out in the day. If all else failed, we were near enough to the sea to catch small flounders on worms.

Flounders are sweet eating, but for every flounder you usually catch two eels. Eels writhe into an unkillable slimy knot with your tackle engulfed somewhere in their coils. If the river failed, there were the animals or the birds. There were no grey squirrels in the bordering woods, only the so-called red, although their tail colour ranged from blonde, through auburn to dark brunette. There were roe deer and capercaillie in the woods. There were hares and partridges in the fields and there were pheasants everywhere. High above us buzzards wheeled and mewed. Dippers bobbed at us in their black and white uniforms from the river's edge. We even found a solitary salmon.

In the middle of this a postcard arrived from the girls bearing the cryptic message 'We've got another one – it's called Star – love C-J. It isn't – it's called Tiddles – love Sue.' Mark and I identified the object of this disagreement as an extra cat. We wondered if it was another stray. Sue had recently come all the way home by train from our friends on Dartmoor with a carrier bag containing a black and white stray, which she had adopted down there. Luckily that stray had deserted us and latched on to another family in the village – thereby sparing us the most fearful swearing matches with our cat. Cats can be very rude to each other. Mark and I put the matter out of our minds for the rest of the holiday.

We drove home from off the night Motorail on a Monday morning. I thought of my colleagues on their way to the start of a new week at the office. 'Where's Star?' Mark asked C-J. 'Where's Tiddles?' I asked Sue. We couldn't resist it. 'In the stable – of course,' replied Sue. She sounded irritatingly pert. I didn't see the 'of course' bit, at all. I should have been warned by the amused glint in Ann's eye. She seemed careful not to join in the conversation. Mark and I went up to the stable. Sitting in the straw and looking up at us curiously with wide eyes and wet grey noses were two Jersey calves – Splash and another one. The mystery was solved.

Shortly after Mark and I had left for Scotland, the two girls had had little difficulty in persuading Ann that Splashdown would need a companion. Otherwise, she would become very lonely when turned out into the paddock just with sheep. Star had been acquired in the same way as Splashdown, and from the same farm. But this time, there had been no incidents on the return journey. Star had cost five pounds also. She was very pretty. Compared with Splash, she would be a dainty little cow. Sue kept the pet name of Tiddles for her, but, officially, she was Star.

The trouble with starting a dairy herd from scratch with calves, is that you have to wait nearly two years before you have milk. Although they start bulling earlier, heifers should not be put in calf until they are at least a year old. Then there is a wait of nine months until the calf is born. During all that time the animal is growing at its owner's expense, with no return. However, once they were weaned from the bucket, Splash and Star were no great economic burden. They grew well on a diet of hay. They were turned out of the stable, spending the winter down in the paddock with Shadow and his young son. They were within easy reach of the house and Sue schooled them on the lawn each day and taught them to lead in head collars.

That schooling came in very handy in the spring, when they joined Angus and Ogilvy and the sheep in Q's field for a short time. It was obvious there was not going to be enough grass to go round, so the heifers were put on their best behaviour in a field, about two miles away, which had been lent to us. Sue and C-J led the heifers along the road, to the great amusement of other road users. The grass in their new field was lush and green. There was a dairy herd two fields away which they could watch. There was a good drinking trough. In fact there was everything that two healthy young heifers could want.

Our telephone rang at two o'clock in the morning. Splash,

lonely for her boyfriends, had jumped the fence and trotted all the way back to Q's field. Unfortunately, she had turned off the road one gate too early. She had created havoc in a neighbour's garden and filled the night air with agonized bellows as she got stuck in the garden hedge trying to force her way through to the bullocks. By the time we arrived on the scene, she had backed out of the hedge and was cavorting around the garden, snorting, kicking and generally eluding capture in a badly behaved way. Sue caught her up and led her all the way back by torchlight. Star was still in the field, standing as good as gold, with her nose pressed through the bars of the field gate.

The next morning Splash did the same again. We seemed to have a fatal habit of acquiring animals with a liking for jumping fences. There was only one solution. Splash was tethered. Sue used a double goat chain to give her plenty of room, but this did not stop her from sulking. Star was quiet and grazed placidly. Splash was generally ill-humoured and roared her discontent between mouthfuls. We were relieved when hay-making was over and we could give that field back again. There had been no complaints, but we were glad to be rid of the uncomfortable feeling that the heifers were overstaying their welcome. Back they went to join everybody else in Q's field.

We decided to join the voluntary scheme for the eradication of brucellosis. It only seemed fair to the farmer who had the land next to Q's field. He had bought a large herd of Jerseys which was accredited as brucellosis free. It would have meant a serious loss for him if his herd had lost their status because one of our little brutes was a carrier. This was most unlikely. The herd they were born into was also accredited. We knew that they had not been in contact with other cattle, except the bullocks. But that was on the assumption that Splash had kept to the road on her two excursions. We decided to play it safe.

And, anyway, if the breeding idea was ever to materialize, it would be essential to sell accredited stock.

The common name for brucellosis is contagious abortion. Not only does it prevent breeding, but milk produced by infected cattle can, if it is unpasteurized, be a health hazard to humans. For the purpose of the scheme, the heifers had to submit to blood tests at prescribed intervals. Also we had to run an inner fence of barbed-wire to create a no-man's-land between Q's field and any adjoining agricultural land.

Creating the no-man's-land took Mark and me one Sunday fence stringing. The Ministry of Agriculture, helpful, efficient and friendly, arranged for a vet to take the first blood samples. The first tests were clear. This was just as well. Splash and Star had turned up in a field of kale the dairy farmer was preserving for his Jerseys. He was very nice about it and conceded that our Jerseys must have a degree of agility way beyond anything he had ever experienced. To get at that kale, the little devils had wriggled under the barbed-wire into no-man's-land. From there they had forded a stream, climbed a steep slippery bank and clambered over a fence of cattle netting. Normally Jerseys can be kept back by little more than a length of string. We were sure that Splash was the ringleader. Star was simply too timid to get up to that sort of prank. It was not as if they were short of forage. It was a combination of curiosity and greed. They had scoffed so much kale, we had to impound them in the field shelter and observe them for a day in case they got bloat or colic.

Bloat is a frightening thing. I have seen it once in a goatling and realized too late what the trouble was. It can be started by a change of diet, usually to an abundance of rich food. Undigested food starts to ferment in the beast's stomach which distends rapidly, due to the resulting gas pressure. The stomach wall, in turn, presses on a nerve centre, causing paralysis in the hindquarters. The animal comes down and death follows very quickly. If you are there in time, the only hope is to plunge a knife straight into the stomach keeping the cut open to release the gases. Even if I had realized what the trouble with that young goat was, I don't know if I would have had the courage to knife it. Splash and Star got away with their over eating. They were lucky.

When they were a year old, Splash and Star were ready to be put in calf. Sue consulted Tony. She had left school in midsummer and had started work with him. She made arrangements through the Milk Marketing Board for artificial insemination with semen from a well-known Jersey bull. There were no suitable Jersey bulls available for service in the area. I was not sorry. Jersey cows are gentle, timid and very effeminate. Jersey bulls are terrors. They are magnificent looking animals, very male, but very unreliable. A friend of mine, a huge man of eighteen stone, was nearly killed by his own bull. He had owned it for years and it had never given any trouble. While the bull was in its exercise pen, its owner got in with it to inspect the guttering on the byre. No sooner had he turned his back, than the bull came silently up behind him, tossed him with a terrific smash into the byre wall and then knelt on him, goring him with his horns. He was in hospital for eighteen weeks with a ruptured spleen, broken ribs, a broken thigh and both forearms broken. I was glad that Sue had settled on artificial insemination for the heifers. I did not fancy her anywhere in the vicinity of a Jersey bull, however competent the handler.

Star held to insemination in late autumn, but Splash returned. She started bulling again. She returned three times and we gave up for the time being. If she had held on the fourth occasion, her calf would have been born too near to winter in the following year, and we did not have the facilities for that situation. The pair of them stayed in Q's field during the winter. In the spring they were put in a secluded orchard of rather less than two acres. We had arranged to have the use of the orchard for grazing, in exchange for a fat lamb a year. We were expanding.

In the May, impatient for our own milk, we bought a large platinum blonde Jersey, called Susie, who had a bull calf called Bossy at foot. Susie and Bossy were installed in another orchard some three miles away. This time the means of exchange was fresh milk. Both lots of cattle had to be bucket watered. Fortunately there were taps nearby in each case. Sue scorched up the roads morning and evening on a rickety old bicycle. Bossy shared Susie's milk with us. Sue milked our share into two miniature churns each morning before going to work. The churns were left under the hedge for collection – one by the orchard owner and the other by us. Cows' milk should be sold to the Milk Marketing Board, but, as far as I know, no regulation prohibits one giving it away as a 'thank you' for grazing.

One morning, I collected our mini-churn by car. I had to brake sharply to avoid a dog. The top flew off the churn and one splosh set the bottom of the car swimming in milk. Once milk has got into fabric, you either have to wait patiently for the awful smell to diminish – it never goes away – or burn it. Washing is better than nothing. We were disinclined to replace the car's carpeting, so we scrubbed and scrubbed and held our noses. On a warm wet day, that car still gives off the faint odour of ripe Stilton. Bossy started getting saucy at an early age. He would come up behind us, playing his boisterous version of 'catch as catch can' as soon as his horns were through. We had no choice but to have him castrated quickly.

Star calved in September, back in Q's field. Sue went in to inspect her one evening and thought at first that a brown dog was in with the cows. It was a small, evenly coloured, brown bull calf. Sue had been hoping for a heifer. 'It's a bum bull,' she told us back at the house –

very fed up. A moment later however she relented, and with a cheerful smile, said, 'I'll have to call him Bumble.'

Susie and Bossy were taken to Q's field to join up with the other three for the winter. Sue had taught Star to accept hand milking, but in November stopped milking both the cows. Bumble was very dependent on Star and Bossy took anything Susie had to offer. The small herd was wintering out and the calves' requirements had to come before ours.

It was a bad winter. It rained and rained. Dry cold does little harm, but rain takes a lot out of animals in the open, even with good shelter available. One morning, shortly after Christmas, we got a frantic message for help from Sue over the telephone of a household near Q's field. Star was down. She had slipped on a muddy slope going down to the stream to drink and had slid into the water. The stream was running quite full and Star was a small cow. She had nearly exhausted herself clambering out of the stream and had gone down on her side again close by.

By the time we got there, Sue had returned to the cow and managed to get her to her feet. The cow was in a bad way – shocked and shivering. Very carefully we led her across to the field shelter. We rubbed her down with sacking, covered her with an old horse blanket, propped her up with straw bales and called the vet. The vet diagnosed exhaustion and gave her a vitamin injection. He told us she would pull through, if we could manage to keep her on her feet. For two days everything went well. Star kept on her feet and ate. On New Year's Eve, Sue and I went to see her in the evening. She was lying down in the straw, with her legs tucked under her in a perfectly normal position. Her eyes were bright and her ears were pricked. She looked so well we were sure the crisis was over. We thought a good night's sleep could do her no harm at all. The next morning she was dead. She had tried to get to her feet in the night, but had failed. Her digestive system had packed up with the usual fatal consequences.

It was a bad start to the new year. Fortunately Susie allowed Bumble to suckle and Bossy raised no objection. By that time, I had ample evidence that, even without the loss of Star, cows were a venture which could not conceivably pay. If Bossy and Bumble were run on to beef, we would avoid loss, with a bit of luck. But that was all.

Susie was due to calve again in the spring and we got a good price for her from a smallholder who wanted a house-cow. Splash had failed to hold to artificial insemination again and again. Our vet thought she would probably only hold to a real live bull. Some cows are like that. So Splash was sold at market into a commercial herd and we lost track of her.

We have never registered the prefix White Rocks, but that pedigree herd remains a gleam in Sue's eye. Once you have had Jersey cows, they get under your skin somehow.

## II

# Chance and Snowy

In recent years, our life has been more than usually full of surprises. A surprise that Providence had reserved especially for me, and which the family has always sworn arose solely out of my own inattention, arrived one Saturday evening. The telephone rang. I picked up the receiver, confirmed to the caller that he was speaking to me, and asked him to identify himself. He did. He told me he was the parcels' clerk at that station 'Ten minutes' walk' from our old house. I can hear his next words even now. 'We have a goat here addressed to you – will you come and collect it, please, before the station closes – that is in half an hour.' I was so startled that all I could think of to do was to say 'Yes – thank you for telling me', and put the telephone down. Having a goat dumped unexpectedly on your lap by telephone would excite anyone and I was no exception.

I bellowed up the stairs for Sue. I had not the slightest doubt that she was at the bottom of that telephone message. Sue appeared at the top of the stairs, uneasily trying to maintain an expression of self-assured unconcern. Ann and C-J were in attendance behind her. From the expression on their faces, it was clear that they shared Sue's uneasiness and wanted to be in the rear rank when it came to braving the matter out. 'Do you know anything about a goat?' I asked. 'Yes,' said Sue stoutly. 'Was that the station?' Sue had learned at a very early age that it paid to pretend that nothing was unexpected or abnormal. 'Why wasn't I told about it?' I asked – keeping my voice down with great difficulty. 'You were,' three voices chorused. Ann and C-J had sensed that Sue had broken through my lines with her single simple counterattack. They were pouring their battalions of feminine innocence and guile through the breach behind her. I was hopelessly out-gunned and out-numbered and, anyway, the goat had arrived and was waiting to be picked up. I could not very well disown it. Ann and Sue set off on the five-mile journey to the station in the Mini.

While they were away, C-J told me that Sue had been saving all the money she had earned from babysitting for neighbours for months past to buy a nanny goat. C-J also repeated her solemn assurance that I had known all about it. I suppose I might have done, but the imminent arrival of a goat is not the sort of thing to slip one's memory. I had an uneasy feeling that I had never participated in that decision and that the three of them had adopted a somewhat pragmatic approach to the truth.

The Mini returned bearing the latest addition to the family – a white female kid, about six months old, of the breed called British Saanen. Sue had ordered her from a well-known firm of livestock dealers. I remarked that buying animals by mail order could turn out to be a chancy business. Sue agreed, but said they were a very reputable firm and promptly named her goat Chance, to show that she was not superstitious.

The stable had recently been vacated by Splash and Star, so there was no problem about sleeping quarters. Sue had already laid in a supply of Dairy-mix – ordered on my account at the local agricultural merchants. It was autumn, and we had plenty of hay laid on. Chance had a house and a supply of food. On warm days she was turned out and tethered on a chain with access to a supply of brambles. Vegetable fibre, the coarser the better, plays an important part in the life of a goat's digestive system.

Chance was unregistered. That is to say she was not eligible for inclusion in the herd book of the British Goat Society. The idea was that she should be mated to a billy of irreproachable pedigree so that her progeny could be registered. If that progeny was female and was mated in turn to a pedigree billy, their produce could be up-graded to the middle rank. A further generation would be required to reach pedigree status. Chance was intended to be the great-grandmother of a small herd of pedigree British Saanen goats. Optimistically, Sue had already chosen the prefix – Wanderers. We thought a trade card advertising both the Wanderers herd of Saanen goats and the Wayward flock of Jacob sheep would look rather nice.

Nanny goats let you know when they are ready for a visit to the billy by altering the pitch of their bleat and wagging their tails vigorously – something like a well-known pop singer. As the autumn days shortened we waited anxiously for those distinctive symptoms. The weeks went by. Chance showed no sign at all of requiring any male attention. Sue looked thoughtful and called the vet. The vet inspected Chance's pink and white posterior and told us that he was almost certain that she was an hermaphrodite. This phenomenon is not uncommon in goats. It occurs in cattle and sheep as well. It is most common in those cases where twins of different sex are born. The presence of male hormones, associated with the male twin, while both are inside the mother, upsets the development of the reproductive organs in the female twin. Our vet advised us that we should take her to the billy, with a normal nanny ready to be covered. There was a remote chance that the billy would cover Chance as well with fruitful results. This would only be the case if her condition was limited to a lack of female mating behaviour at the onset of ovulation and she was normal in other respects.

We did not have another nanny. Sue wrote a reproachful letter to her reputable supplier. It seemed to me that she got a very disreputable reply. Instead of offering Sue a free exchange, they merely hinted at the possibility of a preferential price on the next occasion she bought livestock from them. Sue fumed. I considered the possibility of a very nasty letter. We did nothing. The hard fact was that we had become very attached to Chance. Very few animals are entirely lacking in personality and some animals are real characters. Within a few days of her arrival Chance made it clear that she was one of these. Saanens lack the attractive colouring of other breeds of goat. Their coats are an unrelieved sheenless white and the exposed skin is pink with the odd brown freckle. But they do have highly intelligent faces. As soon as Chance heard us coming up to the stable, she would stand up, resting her forefeet on the stable door and look out at us. If we talked to her, she would listen with a quizzical expression on her face and flick her long white ears back and forth alternately. C-J suggested that we could teach her to talk using her ears as some kind of semaphore system. If we broke off our conversation with her before she had had enough, she would paw chidingly at the door and summon us back with low meaningful bleats.

In the weeks which followed the vet's verdict, when the weather was fine, Chance was taken through the woods and tethered in a field with Tubby – my sister-in-law's pony. From there she could see the footpath. Every passer-by, going for a stroll through the woods, was addressed with an interrogative bleat. It sounded like an indistinctly pronounced 'who goes there?' White goats tethered in a field with a pony are not a usual sight. Goats on self-imposed sentry duty are distinctly uncommon. Chance's capacity for self-advertisement led to two bits of luck.

One Sunday afternoon, when I was digging the vegetable garden by the stable, Sue appeared talking earnestly with two strangers. They were a husband and wife who had been accosted by Chance while walking through the woods. They were standing, entranced with her ear flicking, when Sue appeared to take her home for supper. Apparently they also had a Saanen nanny. They were about to go abroad – the husband had been posted to the Persian Gulf by the oil company which employed him. They were looking for a home for their goat. They were impressed by Chance's quarters. Sue acquired a new goat in exchange for nothing but a promise of kindness. She arrived the next day and gave Sue a very awkward half hour refusing to let down her milk at milking time. She had no name, but Sue called her Mildred.

Sue likes to organize her animals. Mildred did not like being organized. Milking time, night and morning, got them both hot and bothered. It was a battle of obstinate wills. C-J learned her milking on Mildred. The younger girl's tentative and gentle approach produced immediate copious results. Sue was rather put out.

The second bit of luck arose out of my recounting the story of Mildred's arrival to some friends at a dinner party. One of my fellow guests also owned Saanens which she was busy up-grading. She was looking for a home for her original nanny – an unregistered goat in the same category as Chance. Sue followed this up by telephone next day and we collected a large, cantankerous old lady who was already named Snowy.

Snowy was another character. If she liked you everything was fine and she would rub her head and neck against you with low murmurs of approval. If she did not like you, she would half rise from the ground on her hind legs and use her head as a battering ram in a series of vicious butts. If you were really unlucky she would follow up her butts with a painful nip from her teeth. Her likes and dislikes varied from day to day. Visits to Snowy had an air of uncertainty. She never liked being milked, not even by C-J. Although she would let her milk down, she had to be tied up tight in her head collar to save her milker from being nipped.

We were not going to be able to keep three goats in the stable. I set to converting half the adjoining hay barn into goat stalls. I managed this fairly quickly with breezeblocks. We decided to let the earth floor remain. I made two stalls – each one ten foot by six foot and we installed the goats. Snowy – by virtue of her seniority – had a stall to herself. Chance and Mildred shared the other. A few days after we had put them in the stalls, Sue read that goats were very susceptible to draughts. I was persuaded into erecting an inner wooden lining to the stalls of tongued and grooved boarding about five foot high. This would exclude draughts and, because of the cavity walling effect, add warmth in winter and coolness in summer.

One evening I was lining Snowy's stall. She was in an off mood as far as I was concerned. After putting up with a few painful butts and nips, I secured her tightly to a tethering ring. She complained loudly, but I ignored her. Fitting that boarding neatly and snugly was a satisfying job which did not tax my skill greatly. Humming happily to myself, I got on with it, sitting on my hunkers and working from the floor upwards. After a while I realized that Snowy had stopped complaining and turned round with 'good girl' rising to my lips. I came face to face with Snowy looking at me with a sardonic smile in her devilish black and yellow eyes. The tail end of my jacket was hanging out of the side of her mouth. Somehow she had nibbled the knot of her tether undone and, with silent malevolence, had come up behind me and eaten the flap of my jacket off my back, as I worked to increase her comfort. After that act of base ingratitude, Snowy never bothered to butt or nip me again. When I talked to her, she would simply incline her head on one side with a condescending look. I am sure she was saying 'Jackets to you, my friend.'

Snowy and Mildred started tail wagging on the same day in late autumn and, together with a disinterested Chance, were packed into the back of the Land-Rover, which was quite new, and taken to the billy. It was during the week. I was at the office so the job fell on the shoulders of Ann and Sue, who had started her Christmas holidays. When they arrived at the stud, they were taken into a large paddock which contained a substantial wooden shelter. A white donkey came trotting swiftly across to greet them at the gate. Ann – who does not like large animals of any kind – was about to murmur something polite, when she became aware of a pungent male smell. The donkey was a goat – a very large billy goat named Hornet. Hornet covered Mildred and Snowy in quick succession and then, because he was an old hand, unlikely to injure himself by over-exertion, was permitted to go through the same motions for a bewildered Chance. Two satisfied nannys and a complaining outraged Chance were brought home. The Land-Rover was quite new no more. It smelt of Hornet for weeks. We felt we had come to know him intimately.

Chance had a phantom pregnancy. She swelled prodigiously and produced nothing. Sue told me it was an event known in the goat world as a 'cloud burst'. It may have been, but it was of no economic value whatsoever. The vet's suspicions were well-founded. Mildred produced twin billy kids and Snowy produced triplets – one still-born billy, one live billy and one nanny.

Kids are amongst the most beautiful of baby animals. All four of ours had a pair of white toggles hanging from the upper part of their necks. These produced a neat counterbalance to their large white ears, sitting on top of innocent little faces, with pink noses and the most lovely blue eyes. Wobbly on their legs for a day or two, they soon gained strength and pranced around the stalls in real giddy-goat games. They would all stop playing at an un-heard signal and sink to their foreknees under their mothers, butting at the twin titted udders with their snub noses, demanding that milk be let down to them. Chance was aunt to the kids and one of their favourite pranks was to come jumping up to her and bounce off her side with all four legs stiffly extended. If Chance was not available, they would bounce off the stall walls or a bale of straw in ex-actly the same way. At rest time, they would sit in the straw on the floor with their legs tucked neatly under them, gazing up at any visitor with their large trusting blue eyes, and giving forth friendly, high pitched bleats.

The three billy kids were destined for the pot at eight weeks – so Sue did not name them. There is little demand for billys, except from the few breeders who are prepared to keep them. They need plenty of nannys to cover to stop them from going sour and even the most careful manage-ment does not prevent them from producing their very male odour in the mating season.

The nanny kid was named Fancy. She was a pretty little creature and we hoped she would not turn out the same way as Chance. Her brothers went to the slaughter house in due time and, although Snowy's enormous bag was milked dry every evening, Fancy started to grow very fast with the extra food supply.

I will never forget one moonlit night. I was woken by a strange scampering on the path below the bedroom window. I got out of bed and looked out. Snowy and Fancy had climbed out of their stall and were racing backwards and forwards between the stable and the far corner of the house. They would break into their running every now and then, leaping and twisting in mid-air, milk white in the moonbeams. As I watched their elegant movements, I realized the true meaning of the word 'capering'. It comes straight from the word used by the Romans to describe the antics of goats. Like so much ancient language which has survived, it shows how close our forebears were to nature.

Fancy was not an hermaphrodite, and before her first birthday became the bearer of twins herself. Mildred overcame her initial shyness and the obstinate side of her personality developed into a quiet sociable felicity. She became the sober commonsense element in the herd. Poor Snowy trod on her own bag the year after Fancy was born and, despite antibiotics, the cut became badly infected. Her kids were ready to be taken from her and, after consultation with the vet, we put her down. She was very old.

Chance missed Snowy badly and when some other goat owners nearby who were moving to Wales offered to take her down there on loan and use her for eating brambles down, we jumped at it. The firm who sold Chance to us remained very much in our black books.

## 12

# Most Civil Service

Shortly after we took up the offer of Q's field, I had mentioned something of our ideas to Tony. It was a casual cautious mention. Tony had been very understanding at the time of the Orion affair. But I was none too sure how he would react to an extension of our activities. Q's field was very close to Tony's land. Animals do escape and we were blundering around in an amateurish way. Tony was a professional and although not the most industrious of men – he liked his shooting too – he knew exactly 'How many beans make five'. Moreover Sue was angling for the possibility of working for Tony when she left school the following year. But she wanted to stalk Tony by herself, with the rest of us kept well down out of sight. Tony's reaction was friendly but studiously neutral. He neither encouraged nor discouraged. He did murmur something about the possibility of capital grants though. It seemed to me that perhaps it was time to let the authorities know what we were doing and to find out what help was available.

The Rural District Council had been most helpful with the phase one building operation. Moreover, we had a nice friendly relationship going with the rat man. If you keep animals, you cannot avoid rats. As soon as the first frosts come and there are no more gleanings in the fields, our rats arrive. They burrow into the banks of the Frog. They steal the hens' eggs. They grow large and bold and look vicious. Some people have told us that rats are really rather nice creatures. We have never believed them. From the time they first arrived, we hated the rats. To be honest, we were all a bit frightened of them. Rat elimination is covered by our rates and we get our money's worth. The nicest thing about our relationship with our rat man is that he is glad to be called in and is interested in the growth of our activities. Like many people whose work is in the country, he has a fund of knowledge. Ann has extracted a host of useful hints about vegetables from him while he has been in her kitchen, and enjoying a mug of coffee before going on to his next call.

That autumn I wrote to the local office of the Ministry of Agriculture and told them about the sheep, bullocks and heifers, and about our plans for Q's field. I asked them for information and advice. For about six weeks nothing happened and then a large envelope arrived in the morning post. It contained a great deal of information in pamphlet form, some application forms and a long covering letter. The letter was written in simple, friendly language. We were not eligible for any capital grant schemes, because we were not farming commercially. We were eligible for beef calf subsidy and would be encouraged to participate in the voluntary scheme for the eradication of brucellosis in cows. We would have to keep a record of the movements of our animals and, in common with everyone else, inform the authorities of any notifiable diseases.

The beef calf subsidy was worth applying for. It would reduce our investment in the bullocks to approximately nothing. There was one part of the application form which was unclear, so I telephoned the Ministry and asked for clarification. Not only did I get the answer to my question, but a helpful young lady told me that we were the first commuter-belt people in the area who had approached the Ministry for help. She then offered to send us, free, gratis and for nothing, all sorts of helpful information from ways of making cheese, to brine recipes for pickling ox tongues. There was no doubt we had been thought about. Possibly we had been laughed about too, but there was a real willingness to help.

Shortly after, the inspector came to approve the bullocks for subsidy. Sue and I had manhandled Angus and Ogilvy up the hill from Q's field and put them in the stable.

They were still just small enough to be manoeuvred with one hand on a head collar, the other on a tail. It was hard work though. I felt slightly pretentious as I solemnly provided the inspector with a bucket in which to disinfect his boots before and after visiting our solitary agricultural building. He could not have been kinder. He approved the two bullocks, said they were nice beasts, clipped a mark in their ears and told us their probable breeding. He made a complimentary remark about the two heifers. They had been turned out of the stable and were complaining about it. By the time he left we were swollen with self-confidence.

I had approached the Customs and Excise on the possibility of voluntary registration for VAT. It seemed to me that producing your own food ought to rank for favourable consideration for the same sort of reason as building your own house. The initial reply was rather forbidding.

Plainly we were not the first people to approach the Customs and Excise on that subject. We were solemnly warned about the rigorous book-keeping requirements and the awful penalties which would be inflicted on us if we forgot to record the sale of so much as a bunch of flowers. The thought of selling flowers convulsed us. Somebody had missed the point. I came to the conclusion that it was a 'stock' letter and telephoned the official who had signed it. I told him that making Q's field sheep proof was going to be expensive and that I was quite prepared to do the necessary book-keeping to recover the VAT content. I was a bit surprised by his immediate response – 'then you should certainly apply for registration. Later on we'll send someone round to see you.' Our application for registration was accepted, and I started keeping records in the pre-scribed form.

The 'someone' eventually arrived to see us. It was a beastly day, pouring with rain which slanted through the air from scudding clouds blown along by a rising south-westerly gale. The 'someone' was a nice young man who had made an appointment to suit my convenience. He arrived smack on time. After a cup of coffee, we were inspected. We went in for a bit of theatre. Ann pointedly apologized for being busy in the kitchen making bread. I produced a spare pair of wellingtons and some oilskins. And off we trudged. The young man did not quite have the courage to enquire why we could not go to Q's field by car. The elements co-operated. The gale increased. The top of the ridge disappeared into the cloud base, and the road to the field was littered with fallen twigs. Down at the field Angus obligingly looked black and sinister. Ogilvy looked wet and fed up and the sheep were dimly visible sheltering under the trees. The contrast with the dry com-fort of the goats back at the stable – and even the com-parative snugness of the heifers in the paddock – was dramatic. There could be no doubt at all that we were pioneers fighting a hostile environment. The cautious approach, which had been so obvious above the rim of the coffee mug, melted away.

Back home, I was taken enthusiastically through the intricacies of VAT. All sorts of possibilities, which had never occurred to me, were paraded for my education. We were sitting in the dining-room, which I used to enter up our VAT records. It was pointed out to me that, when I came to repaint the room, I would be entitled to reclaim the VAT on a proportion of the paint since the room qualified as my 'VAT Office'. This was co-operation indeed.

Most of the advice I never took. It would have involved a lot of calculation and record-keeping. Moreover, registration under our circumstances involved the authorities in exercising their discretion in our favour. We felt it would be wrong to respond by making hogs of ourselves. Nevertheless, I was very grateful to the young VAT officer for going to such lengths to explain our rights, if we ever wanted to use them.

The crowning glory was the attitude of the Inland Revenue. We hoped to increase our minute sales of breeding stock and we intended to sell any edible produce which was surplus to our requirements to friends at current farmers' prices. It seemed to me that it was most unlikely that this could ever result in a profit. However, for safety's sake, I thought the Inland Revenue should know. The first reaction was so fiercely official that I could only conclude that 'tax loss' farming was not quite the thing of the past I had believed it to be. We would have to keep full annual accounts. I wrote asking for clarification on such problems as valuing and depreciating things we hoped to build ourselves, 'like chicken runs and sheep pens'. After weeks of silence, a short informal letter arrived from the Inspector. He said, 'On reflection I will not require details of your small farming enterprise until your total sales exceed one thousand pounds.' We took great pride in being referred to as 'a small farming enterprise', and by Her Majesty's Inland Revenue – no less.

Our main dealings with those public servants were compressed into a very short period. They were busy with larger matters to attend to. They were very nice people, doing pretty thankless jobs with humour and understanding. The 'small farming enterprise' will always be grateful to them.

# 13

# Workers' Co-operative

Less than a year separated the completion of the stable building and the arrival of the bullocks, heifers and goats. We were getting deeper into the animal business. And more quickly than we had expected. The idea of developing a strategy to help us weather the storm, should inflation get out of control, had been in our minds when we devised the three phase building programme. 'Developing a strategy' was not quite the right description of the rather haphazard way in which animals kept on arriving. We still hankered after dual-purpose animals. The goats could be described as dual-purpose. There is a demand for pedigree goat stock and Sue intended to up-grade our small herd. The same could just about be said of the Jerseys. But we all knew the truth about Angus and Ogilvy. The arrival of those two was as significant as the hatching of Bagpipes and Lady Jane had been. It marked another change in our lives. We became a shade more serious. We also realized the enterprise was becoming so large that before long we would have to work out a more systematic and organized way of running it.

The main fact that any system would have to accept was that the whole thing had to be run in our spare time. Ann split her week between part-time work with disabled children and running the house. There was the usual amount of cooking and shopping. There was an unusual amount of cleaning, washing and darning. Mark was living at home temporarily, working as a ward orderly in a hospital and studying for a second shot at A-level mathematics. Sue was about to start working for Tony. She would help with the Arab horses night and morning. This arrangement would leave Sue with a useful chunk of time in the middle of the day. C-J was at day school some seven miles away and I had my office job in London. We knew that we could call on friends or neighbours to help us out in an occasional dire emergency. We also knew we did not want to. Doing things differently from other people is all right, if you do not make a nuisance of yourself. Anyway, in a nice kind way, the village had already decided we were slightly potty. We had an uneasy feeling they might be right, but we were blowed if we were going to admit it. This element of family pride isolated us somewhat as we put our heads into the wind and got on with it.

So far as was practicable, we divided work between us on the basis of our particular likes and aptitudes. It did not always work that way. Some jobs were just plain unpleasant and we all had to take our turn in doing them. A form of organization based on a pattern of interdependent, self-disciplined work loads gradually evolved. In the main, we had to devise the solutions to our problems for ourselves. We did have books available to us. We devoured

*Farming Ladder* by George Henderson, *The Fat of the Land* and *Self-Sufficiency* by John Seymour and his wife, and others like them. We found the authors' opinions interesting and useful, but by no means infallible. In some cases they were – for our situation – simply impracticable. It would have saved us a lot of disappointment if they had prefaced their avowals of the plain truth with the words 'in the circumstances within my personal experience . . .'

Ann took on responsibility for the vegetable garden and the poultry. She did most of the work and planned the most useful and productive way of running them. Ann also had to cope as best she could with daytime emergencies. This occasionally involved dealing with straying animals when Sue was not about. Ann did not like this at all if they were large ones. She is rather small. If she got in a real jam and Sue was down with the Arabs, Tony was very good about giving Sue temporary release so that she could come and sort things out.

One of Mark's jobs was helping out with any heavy physical work. He disliked it thoroughly, threatened rebellion occasionally, but usually got on with it in a mood of passive resignation. When it came to killing, trussing and plucking birds for the table he took pride in doing a good job in a detached and clinical way. But what really got Mark moving was his task of shooting for the pot. Rabbit and pigeon was a frequent part of our diet.

The welfare of all the animals, except Ann's poultry, became Sue's responsibility. She had direct charge of all the larger animals and did all the mucking out, milking and so on. Sue organized all the mating, shearing, selling, and killing, as well as making sure we complied with the regulations of the Ministry of Agriculture. It was up to her to decide when to call in the vet for any animal. She never took any risks. Sue also made sure that none of the animals in the house got overlooked. For a long time, her 'goodnight' remark to C-J was 'don't forget to feed the cat'.

C-J went through a phase of forgetting that animals need food as well as love.

C-J was relief milker, first reserve and general helper to Ann and Sue. A flair for music had been sparked off in her by Miss Fitch and practice kept her inside a fair bit. She liked doing her share of cooking. That gave Ann more time for her vegetables. C-J also kept me company from time to time. It was nice to have her chattering away while I was repairing fencing, even if she did keep dropping the staples.

My job consisted of the money side and planning everything to do with the land and buildings. I looked after all the buying of materials – except feeding stuff which Sue arranged – and did the bulk of the heavy work like building and fencing. Sue and I had to work more closely together than the others. Land management goes very closely with animal management. But, by and large, we all worked in harmony and found out how to help each other without neglecting our main duties. Unless it affected the running of the house – which was Ann's province – I had the last word in the rare cases of family dispute. We became a sort of workers' co-operative, with me as the chairman with a small 'c'.

We had to devise ways of overcoming our lack of manpower and lack of knowledge. We could hire help for specialized and dangerous jobs like tree felling. Sometimes we had to call in a helpful friend who is a wizard at sorting out machinery. We are all hopeless at it. Ann and C-J don't want to know, Mark thinks he does and Sue is always game for a bit of trial and error. For my part, if a piece of running machinery starts to make an unusual noise, my first instinct is to steal quietly away from it. But, in general, we had to work out solutions to our problems for ourselves. A bucket of nuts and a herring net as a way of rounding-up sheep was fairly typical of our approach.

It was not long before our self-confidence and proficiency grew. The sheep were still brought running by the rattle of the nut bucket. But the herring net was replaced by a properly constructed fold. Ann tried out a labour-saving way of breaking new ground. She laid potatoes on the un-dug surface in rows and covered the lot six inches deep in stable manure. She needed help to cart the manure, but the technique gave us, and many of our friends, wonderful potatoes in a terrible drought year when conventional methods produced no crop to speak of at all. It also gave us a new fertile vegetable patch, which only needed to be stirred up with a hoe. Very few weeds were able to penetrate that depth of stable manure and the worms, in their turn, took the humus deep into the soil beneath. Digging was quite unnecessary. It cropped the year after the potatoes as if it had been cultivated since the time of Good Queen Bess.

Sue was never short of enthusiasm or self-confidence. The animals gave her a lot of hard work. She established a rough routine for feeding, milking and inspection which the animals all knew. The rest of us knew it too. Back-up arrangements in a timetable that was not too tight were important. The animal timetable had to have some slack in it to leave room for dealing with emergencies. If an animal was sick or straying it had to be given priority. Sue taught all her showing and milking animals – as well as many destined for sale as breeding stock – to walk obediently in a head collar. This saved Sue an enormous amount of time. Time was the commodity we had the least of. Any new approach to a problem, however unorthodox, was worth investigating if it would save us time.

Whereas Sue always liked to work animals to meet her disciplinary requirements, Mark has preferred to adapt himself to the natural behaviour of animals. This instinct soon made Mark a deadly hunter. Long hours of watching animals in the wild had given him a highly developed second sense. Set Mark behind a pile of logs on the flight path of homing pigeons and he can predict their movements with uncanny accuracy when they are still a good two hundred yards away. Professional pigeon shooters know that this is only achieved as a result of long hours getting stiff and cold in the hostile dusk. On wet and windy evenings, large bags only fall to experience. The same techniques applied when Mark was out shooting with Tippy. Tippy coursed the ground in front of him and Mark judged where the rabbit or pheasant was likely to appear by the movements of the eager little terrier. Tippy adores Mark. She adores Mark with a gun even more. The bounces and yelps on the front doormat when Mark appears with his gun and wearing his jacket stained with blood-rust leave no room for doubt about that.

I also worked out ways of doing things. One weekend, when I was shoring up the roof of the small shelter in Q's field, I discovered that a small hydraulic car-jack worked with one foot could, when applied to a propping beam, take the place of the strongest and most reliable companion. I had an advantage over the others in that I have always been able to work for long periods, expending a lot of energy with relatively little sleep. The only snag about this was that I was usually still up when some night-time emergency arose. I do not know if I was more accident prone than the rest of the family or whether they simply kept quiet about the occasions when they fell on their noses. A lot of my misfortunes were due to too much imagination and too little foresight. I still have uncomfortable memories of working into the small hours, the night before Ann was due to return from a holiday, dismantling a combination hay-rack cum feeding-trough which I had constructed during her absence, from timbers saved from the old sheds. It was a beautiful design. For my own comfort I had rolled back the sitting-room carpet and carpentered indoors. The sawdust was soon swept up, but I had forgotten to measure the width of the sitting-room door.

One consequence of our changing way of life was that we had to start splitting our holidays. Some times of the year, when a lot was on, came to be accepted as unavailable for any of us. When things were slack – and we soon learnt how to predict those times – never more than two of us were away together and rarely for more than two weeks at a time. Fortunately Ann and I have always liked different kinds of holiday. Ann likes warmth, rest and company, with some quiet spinning or knitting to keep her occupied. I like to be energetic in the solitude of the north where the air is sharp and the sun is bright, but only warms the back of one's neck and never scorches. C-J often went away with Ann. Mark liked to go off with me. Sue often went down to our friends on Dartmoor, she learnt a lot from them. We have all needed our holidays. The absorption of spare time in a constructive way is very satisfying. I have found the contrast with work at the office particularly refreshing. But the pace of our life is hot and every now and again complete relaxation, doing nothing but enjoy oneself with no responsibilities at all, is an absolute must for all of us.

# 14

# Horseplay

You either get on with horses or you do not. Ann and Mark do not. They like watching them, they like betting on them, but they thoroughly dislike handling or riding them. To be fair, they both had a go at it. Mark has a deep interest in bloodstock – from the right distance. Ann might be persuaded to sit on a fat pony – guaranteed to do no more than walk – and go for a gentle plod through the woods. Mark might be persuaded to go with her. But no more than that – for either of them.

Sue has had a passion for horses since she was very small. She is by no means a daring rider though. She has a well-developed sense of self-preservation and will not take what she considers unnecessary risks with any animal. She had a pony as soon as she was large enough to look after it. The pony was an iron grey Connemara mare named Pretty Thing. I nicknamed her Dingus. Sue nicknamed her Thing. Pretty Thing was altogether too prissy a name for the liking of either of us. We bought Pretty Thing when Sue was nine, one year after we moved house. She was kept at some riding stables near the old house. Sue had helped out at those stables from the time the owner was prepared to tolerate her. The place swarmed with earnest, bright-eyed, grubby little girls. Most of them – like Sue – had already learnt to ride at another stables which kept small shaggy ponies and nothing more. Sue had learnt a lot about the care of ponies by the time we fell for Thing.

Thing was already at the stables and had been up for sale for some time. Her breeder let the owner of the stables, who has a great gift for teaching disabled children, use the pony. It is remarkable to watch the behaviour of his ponies. Some of them can be absolute little devils in an ordinary lesson. But as soon as they have a disabled child on their backs, they are docile and careful. To begin with a helper walks alongside each pony which carries a disabled child. But any disabled child who acquires balance and confidence and can be left safely alone, is set free. The lift that experience gives those children shines from their faces. On the ground, some of them can hardly walk un-aided.

Thing was a particular favourite with those children. When we bought her, we arranged that for a time the disabled children should continue to have the use of her while we paid for half her keep. That lasted until Sue could scrape time together for a ride every day. Sue adored Thing and thought she was perfect. The truth of the matter was that left to her own devices the pony thought twice about even the smallest jump. There were no problems if Thing was given a lead. Out on a drag hunt, careering along behind the fieldmaster, she flew over everything, but out by her-self, no amount of coaxing made any impression. Sue used to be able to persuade her to take the most enormous leaps over jumps about a foot high. That pony imagined that tigers lay in wait below everything that stood above ground level. We have a photograph of Sue, with her eyes tight shut, and her jaw set, perched on top of Pretty Thing whilst she clears a nine-inch mini-jump by about three feet. After four years, when Sue was thirteen, she grew out of Thing and we sold her. She has been owned since by a number of families in the neighbourhood who wanted a safe ride for children to learn on – up to the jumping stage.

Next we bought Andy – Orlando was his grandiose full name – a dark bay gelding. Buying him was probably a mistake. Letting Sue keep him near the house by himself was certainly a mistake. Andy was a lightly built three-quarter bred who had been spotted on a farm up in York-shire by a woman who stabled a horse where Sue kept Thing. That woman had a good eye for a horse. Andy was a real smasher with a lovely action. He was four years old and unbroken. On our visits to Thing, Sue and I watched the process of backing him with interest. It was taken slowly and carefully. Some six weeks lapsed between a saddle be-ing laid lightly on his back and the day when he was led carefully round the school with an experienced girl sitting relaxed and still on him. Andy never put a foot wrong. He seemed to have a perfect temperament. Six months after his arrival we bought him.

Sue was anxious to have him at home and I saw no harm in it. Ann was not keen at all. She agreed finally on the understanding that whatever emergency arose in Sue's absence she would not be required to do more than tele-phone for help. Everything went smoothly for a few months. Andy spent some time in the paddock and some time in a two-acre field near to us and temporarily empty. Andy was a bit lonely for company, but there was enough going on round him to stop him going sour through boredom.

One day Sue came back from a ride through the village. She was white faced and Andy was prancing around like a stallion and snorting with his tail held high. He was barely under control. Both of them were in a state. After a lot of probing I got the story out of Sue. She had not taken Andy down to the village for some time. She had followed her usual route, stopping to talk to two donkeys that Julia kept in the forge garden on the way. Some horses are scared of donkeys but Andy had never objected to those two. Shortly after Julia's house the road begins its rise up from the village to the crest of the ridge. It starts as a gentle slope and gradually gets steeper and steeper. All the riders in the neighbourhood use that hill to muscle up their horses. Sue had just left the donkeys when Andy stopped, snorted and stood still. He was shivering and looking into the field next to Julia's house. There was nothing moving in the field whatever. Sue urged him on. He locked his legs and refused to budge. When Sue used her crop on him he squealed and stood up on his hind legs. The road was slippery and this was a situation Sue had never run into before. Unnerved, she dismounted. It was only with great difficulty that she led Andy past the spot. When she tried to remount, Andy played her up. She eventually got up, but he gave her a bad ride all the way home, spooking and prancing about in the road.

I went down to the village to look for the cause of the trouble. There was no livestock in the field. There was nothing flapping about. Nothing that should have bothered Andy in that way at all. From Sue's description the horse had been badly frightened. There was something about that field though. Then I got it – good and strong. Pigs. I dimly remembered one of the legends that surrounded Julia. At some time past the owner of that field had applied for permission to build on it. The village, with Julia prominent in its front ranks, had objected. The objection was upheld and planning consent refused. The would-be builder said nothing. He simply made his point by spreading periodically a few loads of pig manure about the place. By the time I heard the story, those loads had grown in the telling. Julia had been threatened with asphyxiation in a house besieged by mountains of pig manure. But undoubtedly there was fresh pig manure on that field and its smell was being carried to the road on the breeze. That was what had upset Andy. It was a strong animal smell. It might have been entirely new to him. It might have reminded him of some bad experience on that Yorkshire farm.

The incident ruined the relationship between Andy and Sue. Sue's nerve had gone. She knew it and Andy knew it. He turned in one day from a nice ride for Sue into a torment. It was my fault for letting Sue take on a youngster as her first horse without guidance. The step from a pony to a horse is bigger than many people realize. Particularly if the horse has some hot blood in it. The only thing to do was to sell Andy quickly. Sue was relieved, fond as she was of him, she knew the situation was beyond her. She swallowed her pride and agreed he had to go. It was all a question of confidence between horse and rider. The youngster who took Andy on never had any trouble. The horse went willingly for her.

Andy's place was taken, in the year I put the stable up, by a lop-eared thoroughbred bay gelding called Pepe. His real name is Never Surrender. The son of a very illustrious racing father, he was taken out of racing as a two-year-old with a weak back. Although he is a big horse, the weakness has persisted and he can only carry a girl's weight. Pepe is the soppiest horse I have ever met. If he is told to stand still, while he is unmounted, but has his saddle and bridle on, he just shades the sun from his eyes with his ears and goes to sleep. Sue has never had a bad ride out of him. Pepe lives most of the year in a field Sue rents from Tony. But when the hay crop is taken from Q's field, Pepe joins the sheep. He and Shadow adore one another and Pepe becomes the flock godfather. If we take strangers into the field he positions himself between us and the flock steaming up and down with high blowing and a great flashy trot.

Shortly before we bought Pretty Thing, I decided to learn to ride so that I could keep up with Sue. Each lesson lasted a full hour. After about forty minutes I always had a nasty pain in my hips, and was unable to keep my balance. Jumping was saved until the end of the lesson. I fell off eighteen times in twelve lessons. I fell off in every conceivable way. It was not long before I managed to crack a rib. Our doctor was not the least interested in the rib. But he was intrigued to know why I was falling off. So was I.

An X-ray showed that I had a dose of arthritis in both hips. The tops of both femurs were going nicely egg-shaped and the bearing surfaces of the pelvis showed granulated patches. A cheerful consultant told me that – short of surgery which he did not recommend as I was too young – there was nothing to do but keep the joints exercised. 'Keep on riding, old chap,' he said, 'but don't fall off.' Following that advice required careful timing. On average, it took ten minutes between the onset of pain, after a half hour in the saddle, and complete immobility in the hips when the muscles surrounding the joints locked solid.

I continued with riding lessons for a time. But it was neither very satisfactory for me, nor fair to my instructor. I wanted to go along at my own pace – be it faster or slower – it was more often the latter – than the rest of the class.

The only solution was to acquire a horse of my own

and ride it by myself. I had two false starts over some five years with charming but experienced animals who had fixed habits and wills of their own. The second of them would go weak at the knees and vibrate slowly in a sort of stationary rumba when I scratched his rump with a curry comb. I could get him to do little else at my bidding though. I decided finally to have a go at teaching a horse how to accommodate itself to my requirements. This meant buying a young horse with a quiet temperament, which had been broken, but was otherwise uneducated.

A friend of mine who knows about horses understood the nature of the problem and kept an eye open for something suitable. On her advice I bought Neptune. An Irish hunter, a grey gelding of sixteen hands, he had been backed but little more. He was four years old. When I first sat on him and asked him to turn a corner, he answered the rein by turning his head to look at me, but ignored my feeble leg aids altogether. The rather alarming result was that we trotted along looking like a lopsided banana threatening to fall over. For about a year I borrowed my ex-instructor's indoor school. Usually it was late at night after he had finished with it. I taught Neptune myself, following the books as best I could, but adapting them to my physical problems. I used to work Neptune on the longe for about ten minutes before I mounted him. He spent the first few moments on the longe intent on letting off steam with bucks and snorts. After that he settled down to a nice rhythmic trot. The two most important things I had to teach Neptune were to stand stock still while I clambered on and off him and to stop moving at once if I took the pressure off his mouth and said 'Whoa Boy'. It took a full six months of this schooling before I had the nerve to venture out with Neptune into the open spaces.

I kept Neptune at those stables for a year and then started to look for a field where he could live out. It would be a lot cheaper and much better for Neptune. It was the spring of the year in which Q offered us his field. Sue was looking for spare land. If possible, she wanted a field where it would be safe to put Shadow. A friend of hers from school was looking for a companion for her horse. So it was that we met Jo and Rodney – the parents of Sue's school friend. They lived only four miles from us in a converted groom's cottage. They had a six-acre field in which Rodney had erected a small stable block of two loose boxes and a tackroom. Their daughter's young horse – a pretty chestnut gelding with two wall eyes and powder-blue eyelashes – was already installed and lonely. It did not take Rodney and me long to agree that Neptune would be a more suitable companion than Shadow. What use could a ram have for that lovely cool stable anyway? Sue saw the point quite readily and Neptune was installed. He had everything a horse could want. The only snag was that I could only ride him for about forty minutes at a time. To make his life a bit more interesting for him, we entered some dressage competitions that summer, at beginner's level. Neptune nearly always got somewhere near half marks. The comment from one judge on our performance was 'a kind horse, who is very obedient, but does not go forward sufficiently due to the restricting influence of his rider'. Neptune and I thought that those words described the basis of our relationship with tact and accuracy.

C-J was quite a little girl when Sue started with Pretty Thing. She did not seem all that interested. One day she startled me by asking 'If I stop biting my nails – can I have a pony?' 'But you don't bite your nails,' I replied. 'I know,' she said, 'but I soon could – that's how Lucy Jones got hers.' C-J spent years trying to blackmail us into the purchase of a pony. The issue was fairly easily avoided. She made it clear that she was more interested in looking after a pony than riding it. My 'ponies are for riding' line seemed a pretty good defence.

One day when I was on holiday, I met C-J off the school

bus. She was thirteen and for C-J, Miss Fitch was a distant memory. No sooner was she in the car than she asked, 'If someone gave me a pony – could I keep it? He's called Seamus, by the way.' From the happy twinkle in her eyes, it was clear she thought she had won at last. The process of extracting her explanation of the offer of a free pony gave me time to think. 'If the vet says it's safe,' I said, 'you can have it, provided you can find a field to keep it in and pay to have it shod out of what you earn from baby-sitting.'

I did not want to take the chance away from her. The pony Tubby had been put down the previous spring. She had been off work for a long time and had been getting that strange square-headed look that one sees so often in very old ponies that are gradually failing. C-J had looked after Tubby in the last few months before my sister-in-law decided it was kinder to put the old mare down. C-J had really missed her. On the other hand C-J had to demonstrate acknowledgement that the pony would be an extra for her. We had always tried to treat the children roughly equally in their share of the family budget for hobbies. C-J was not the length of a pony – even a free one – behind the other two.

Seamus was a source of embarrassment from the beginning. A stocky, Irish dun pony of fourteen and a half hands, aged ten, he belonged to an Irish woman who taught at C-J's school. Her daughter had grown out of the pony and a sale had fallen through because the animal had failed to pass the vet. The trouble was said to be an irregular heart beat indicating a deficient valve. Our house has a good reputation for taking care of animals and so C-J was approached. I wanted a separate report on that heart beat before we proceeded at all. Our own vet visited Seamus. He telephoned me at home that evening. 'The pony is as sound as a bell – he's fit for any work.' C-J agreed with me that to sit quiet on that report was only a whisker away from stealing. So we telephoned the owner. She was adamant. She had found Seamus a good home and that was that. I persuaded her finally, in her own interests, to call in a third vet. His verdict cleared Seamus as well. The owner still said an offer was an offer and Seamus was to be C-J's for nothing. I could not have that, and paid her what seemed to me to be a reasonable sum. I told C-J that the purchase price was a debit against the account of my conscience and not against her babysitting fund. But the basic conditions I had laid down had to stand.

My reference to babysitting was a big mistake. C-J is in great demand as a babysitter and an endless number of families were willing to offer Seamus board and lodging at the bottom of their gardens for a couple of weeks at a time.

One of the families lived next door to Julia. One Sunday morning Seamus was missing. There was a notice pinned to Julia's gate. It read 'Will the owner of the brown pony which is in my garden, please collect it.' Seamus had taken a fancy to Julia's donkeys and jumped in. C-J embarrassed Ann by giggling all the way through church.

Hauling Seamus from back garden to back garden, when he would not lead for C-J, became a wearisome and time consuming operation. Finally C-J found a field – all six acres of it. We mentioned that we were already using other land on a sort of barter basis. The field's owner and his wife were intrigued by the idea of getting some grass-fed beef and seeing it grow on their own land – so an understanding was reached. C-J agreed to accept the task of looking after two bullocks in the summer as an additional part of her bargain with me. Seamus had a taste for jumping out of fields. Most households in the village had already met him as an inquisitive trespasser. To our relief, this was cured eventually by the company of Chance when she came back from her stay in Wales. C-J took the hermaphrodite goat under her wing in that field as well.

Seamus has stamped his personality on the family. Shortly after C-J had acquired him, she rode him through the woods – he is a jolly nice ride – to show him off to my sister-in-law. The back door to my sister-in-law's cottage is set a bit below ground level and is approached by a sloping path. Seamus was led up for approval. He allowed his muzzle to be stroked in best pony fashion. At the same time he stiffened his tail, spread his hind legs, leant forward and pissed a foaming cascade of yellow urine down the steps and through the open door. Pony pee is strong smelling. My sister-in-law has never forgotten nor forgiven. She likes ponies, but that was too much.

# 15

# Hay Fever

The one job we all dread is hay-making. It has to be done successfully under the combined pressure of time and the possibility of irreparable damage from unexpected weather changes. None of us likes hay-making time and we do not believe anybody who says he does. However good the weather, we resist the temptation of cutting in June. Generally, there is still so much sap in the stems that there is a risk of overheating in the rick. Hay made successfully in June is of superb quality, but, if it overheats, it spoils and fire can break out if the rick is not quickly dismantled. The larger the rick, the more the risk multiplies and it can go 'critical' in the middle, like a homemade nuclear reactor, without one knowing until it is too late. Our hay-rick is housed in the new barn at the east end of the vegetable garden. The thought of half of phase two going up in smoke gives us all the heeby-jeebies.

At the beginning of July, we start looking anxiously at the weather forecast and the Atlantic charts. Ideally, we need two weeks of settled weather. Wind is helpful. Even a little rain after cutting does not do much harm. After baling, a fair bit of rain is not a cause for much worry, provided it is followed by some good drying days. The real horrors are the isobars of low pressure which wriggle their way north across the Channel from France. When we have hot weather in the South of England, they often cause torrential thunder rain which devastates a hay-crop after it is cut. That sort of rain can cause havoc in a crop that is already baled, as well.

When we think the weather men have got the forecasts right, we contact Tink. Tink was born in Suffolk. He is a small brown man with a soft burr in his voice. He has a gentle sense of humour which twinkles through his eyes and has a fund of helpfulness in him. We were one of the first households to give him work and recommend him to friends when he started his own contracting business. He has never forgotten and, if we are in a real jam, we know Tink will help us out if he can. He has come a very long way from when we first knew him, cutting down brambles with a sickle in his hand and a sack on his back to keep the rain off. A reputation for reliability and careful buying of second-hand machinery were the foundation of Tink's business. He worked harder for his success than almost anyone I know. Out in the open Tink always wears a cloth cap. It is part of his equipment. It keeps off the sun and rain and, at the end of a job, is pushed to the back of his head as a signal of success. I have seen him capless in our house on many occasions, but he always looks a bit undressed and I cannot summon up a mental image of him without one.

Tink usually needs three days' notice to cut the hay. With good drying weather, and a thick crop, another four days at least is needed for turning and rowing up for baling. Baling is completed in one day, and if the weather is right, we like to leave the bales curing in the field for another two days before we cart and stack. In those two days, Sue checks each bale by hand for heating up. If we get rain and the bales get really wet, Sue turns each one to speed up the drying process. That is a back-breaking task. I book a day's holiday away from the office for carting and stacking, on the assumption that everything will go according to plan. It has on one occasion only.

The year we got Angus and Ogilvy brought home to us the importance of growing our own hay-crop and getting it in somehow. It was a wet summer. It rained and went on raining. It was cold as well. We listened to the farmers complaining. We watched the grass grow long and rank in the hay-fields. When the end of July came and no hay to speak of had been made in the area, we began to get nervous. We had two horses, two calves and the sheep to provide for. Moreover, part of the field sharing arrangement with Rodney was that I would lay on hay for his horses as well. With the possibility that there would be more animals still by winter, we needed five tons of hay to be on the safe side. We sometimes got long periods of snow-covered ground. Feeding hay to animals night and morning runs through the bales at an alarming rate. We knew that if there was a shortage, we could be in serious difficulties. The farmers would have none to spare and the merchants would have a bonanza. Our fears grew when Sue told us than Tony was getting worried too. Hay – and a lot of it – was an absolute must for him.

I telephoned our friends in Dartmoor and asked what the situation was down there. They had had more sun than we and a fair quantity of hay had been made. I asked them to buy in eight tons for us and sit on it. If a hay shortage did not develop in the South-East, we could ask them to arrange a re-sale. Any loss, within reasonable limits, that we might make would be a worthwhile insurance premium. We had bought peace of mind and watched the development of local events with equanimity.

The weather did not improve. The hay harvest never got off the ground. Those farmers who did cut and went on turning in the hope that there would be a number of consecutive drying days, sooner or later, were mostly disappointed. In some cases they were able to avoid a total loss by putting cattle into the fields to salvage something from the blackening rows. Some farmers made a small amount of poor stalky hay, but most did not even bother to cut. By October, hay and feeding straw were being imported into the South-East in large quantities. Some retail fodder merchants were quoting hay at £1.75 a bale to customers who wanted small quantities. That was above one hundred pounds a ton. What little was on offer soon went – even at that price. Some horse owners who had been used to relying on friendly farmers became frantic. At a pinch, sheep and cattle can get by quite well on a diet of barley straw supplemented by concentrates, grain and feeding blocks. Horses cannot – they need hay.

In November, we decided to bring our Dartmoor hay up. The one small bonus resulting from the dreadful weather was a large flush of autumn grass. There was a lot of it and it was pretty coarse. It did not hold much nourishment, but it did provide bulk. Bulk is important to all grazing animals. Without it they are prone to severe digestive troubles. It was a long green autumn. The frosts held off. The trees kept their leaves and that grass lasted well.

We found a haulage contractor with a fleet of articulated trailers who made occasional trips down to Cornwall. As soon as he told us he had an empty return run coming up, we booked it. The driver was instructed to take his trailer to the public car park in Moreton Hampstead, and await our arrival. I took a day's holiday from the office and Rodney did the same. Mark had not yet started his job as a ward orderly, and one of our friends who had helped with the phase one building was available as well. I had telephoned our Devon friends the night before and they had told us that on no account should we attempt to reach them with the trailer. They had a hay platform already hitched up to their tractor and the hay would be ferried to Moreton Hampstead on that.

We left before dawn. It was a bad drive. The rain was coming in from the south-west in great wet curtains. It was so heavy that Stonehenge, normally easy to see from the A303, was nearly obscured from our view as we swished past through the puddles. We reached the trailer in five hours. It was a colossus. Our friends had been quite right. It would have difficulty in negotiating most minor roads, let alone the lanes which crawl tortuously up the sides of Dartmoor. A nasty thought occurred to me. The trailer would get nowhere near us at home either. Still, there would be time to think about that problem after we had got it loaded up.

Our friends live in a small granite-built house stuck on the corner of a quadrangle of squat farm buildings. The Dartmoor granite is very near the surface of their land. The prevailing weather is wet and windy. Their sheep, cattle and horses need a lot of ground to keep them going. It is a pretty gruelling life, but they are very happy. The farm barely keeps itself, so they supplement their income by taking holidaymakers in the summer and any part-time clerical jobs that are going, within reasonable distance, in the winter.

Over a cup of coffee we surveyed the situation. If we used the tractor and hay platform, the bales would get saturated on the way to the trailer. The only solution was to use our friends' van. The bales were big and heavy. They ran about forty to the ton, as against the normal sixty.

There was no doubt that they had been made in the water meadows in the valley far below. The backbone of a Teign salmon, washed over the banks as a spent fish in the spring floods, was stuck to the outside of one bale.

There were six of us. There were some three hundred bales of hay. At best, we could cram fifty bales into the back of the van at a time. That weight put a dangerous strain on the springs. One of us drove the van while the other five followed its soggy, swaying journey down the hill in the car. The inhabitants of Moreton Hampstead were fascinated. They had never seen anything like our emergency hay lift. I do not think they are likely to again.

We were finished in time for a very late lunch. We were wet through and itching, with our eyes streaming from the combined effects of dust and hay-seeds. But we were triumphant. We had accomplished the first part of a very unusual endeavour. We thanked our friends for their help and hospitality, sent our hay on its way to Wincanton, where it would spend the night, and set off home.

The size of that trailer was a problem. There was no chance at all of getting it anywhere near our house. The following morning I cobbled together a plan. A farmer, for whom Sue did relief milking occasionally, had a field bordering a decent sized road about two miles from us. I arranged to rent a corner of that field for a day and bought a large plastic rick sheet to keep our precious hay dry. Rodney and our other friend were not available that day, so Mark and I were landed with the job of unloading the trailer and making a temporary hay-rick. It was the third time we had handled those bales. We were getting to know some of them personally – as Mark kept on telling me.

On the third day the other two were available again, but poor Mark was completely out of action with hay fever. His nose was streaming and his eyes were so puffed up he could hardly see out of them. Our animal trailer was brought into use. It took thirty bales at a time and the loads were carted off to their various destinations. By the time we had finished, each bale had been handled five times in three days, and had travelled more than two hundred and fifty miles. But it was worth it. We made sufficient profit, on the three tons we sold, to cover the cost of hiring the driver and trailer. And the friends we sold those three tons to were glad to have them. Some people sold their horses that year for lack of fodder.

We had our hay that winter at Dartmoor July price. But it was still too expensive. If the animals were going to make any sort of economic sense we would have to make our own hay. Since then four acres of Q's field have been cropped for hay each year. And each year we are on tenterhooks until the crop is in. One year I worked on, singlehanded and furry-tongued, until four o'clock in the morning and a red dawn had turned into a dull grey day, to get the bales uncarted from the previous day under cover before an unexpected weather change overtook us. The family had given it 'best' and packed in at midnight. At between sixteen and twenty pounds a ton, after paying Tink a fair rate for his work and costing our labour as worth nothing, our hay-crop is an essential part of our small economy.

## 16

# Cundy de Barker

In the year that we had planned to start phase two, the inflation that had threatened really arrived. It was not only at a high rate, it was gathering pace in an alarming way. I began to wonder how long the economy could hold up. My private guess was that the roof would fall in if the rate of inflation exceeded thirty per cent a year. It was difficult to see what was going to stop it. We decided to prepare ourselves to deal with a short term economic siege. Serious national difficulties with disruption of supplies lasting any length of time would dish us in the same way as everybody else. But a bit of extra effort would convert our work over the previous two years into some sort of dam – albeit a thin-walled one. The whole family developed a sense of urgency.

This was more than a matter of living an interesting life in the country. We built up a strategic reserve of clothing for each member of the family. Jeans, wellington boots, and plenty of warm woollen garments were laid in. I remembered from the war that one could put up with a lot of discomfort for a long time, if one was warm and dry. So heavy clothing was given priority. We were well provided for food. Meat lived all round us. There were our own animals and the wild ones in the fields and woods. We bought an extra supply of cartridges for Mark to use with the shotgun. We had eggs and milk and plenty of vegetables. To make the best of all this we needed our deep-freeze. But there was no point in a deep-freeze without the means of keeping it going if we lost mains electricity. We bought a one-and-a-half-kilowatt portable generator as a standby.

Phase two of the building programme was completed uneventfully. It was hard work, but I was quite confident about bricklaying and I had two level sites to work with. This time I hired a small cement mixer at the weekends, and arranged in advance for help with erection of the buildings. Mark and a friend worked flat out digging trenches for the foundations. We started in the March and both buildings were up by the end of July. The barn by the vegetable garden received the first hay-crop which we took off Q's field. One section of the building which replaced the garage was intended to house small pieces of machinery and tools. The other section could hold any larger machines we acquired and timber for building the lean-tos of phase three.

We already owned a double trailer which was designed to carry horses, but which would also take cattle, sheep, timber, hay and anything bulky. We acquired a small eight-horsepower tractor early in the year. The tractor had attachments for rotary tilling, grass cutting and power scything. It also pulled a small trailer. That little tractor was invaluable during the building operation, saving time and effort carting materials about.

What had already started to worry us, before the buildings were up, was the problem of food, in an emergency, for the animals. So long as there was grass and hay we did not have too much of a problem. But ideally we wanted crushed grain and concentrates for the milking goats at all times and as a supplement for the other animals in bad times. And there were the horses. They would need crushed grain if we ever had to put them to work. The dogs and the cat would manage as they usually did, on their own scavenging, on offal and on our scraps. The family had their hands full already. The problem was put firmly on my plate. What I needed to find was a small chaff-cutter and a miniature oat-crusher. I soon realized that a hand powered chaff-cutter was a possibility. But a hand powered oat-crusher was absolutely out. It was going to be difficult enough to find a small belt-driven crusher. If I found one that was small enough to be housed in our new machinery building, we would be able to run it. The Land-Rover had a diesel engine and was equipped for power take-off. But small machinery is scarce. I was beginning to realize the rate at which heavy modern mechanization has moved the use of land away from the reach of people working it on a small scale.

After several weeks of useless scanning of 'Agricultural For Sale' columns in the local newspapers, I mentioned the problem to Jo and Rodney. When Neptune moved into their field, Rodney and I had devised a programme for sharing the work of looking after the two horses. A lot of the work fell on the shoulders of Rodney's younger daughter. Late night inspection and – in winter – filling hay-nets and water buckets was my share. I often used to drop in for a chat with Jo and Rodney after I had dealt with the horses. Their house was always spotless – quite unlike ours

– and I used to feel rather guilty about the trail of hay-seeds I left behind me on my late evening calls. They never complained though – not while I was there anyway. They were good friends and very level headed. Their reactions to our plans, as I unfolded them, had been an excellent barometer. The barometer scale ranged from possible, through foolish and very foolish to wildly impracticable. Rodney passed a catalogue over to me. Jo watched me speculatively. It was for an agricultural auction, going on under the rather grand name of a 'Collective Farm Sale'. There were all sorts of things in that catalogue and under the heading 'Collectors Items' I found two chaff-cutters. There was no sign of an oat-crusher under any heading. There were a number of items such as root-slicers and circular saws which might come in useful as well.

I arrived at that sale with a pronounced inferiority complex. The roads leading to the large open field in which the sale was to be held, were jam-packed with farm vehicles of every description. Every vehicle held ruddy-complexioned people with an air of knowing precisely what they were about. They were all in immensely good humour. They had forgotten about inflation for the day. But the more they laughed and joked, as we crawled along in a fog of diesel fumes, the more I felt an intruder.

The auctioneers were running three rings. The articles to be auctioned in each ring were laid out on the ground in long lines with numbered pegs. The starting times were staggered. One ring was to start at 10 a.m., the next at 11.30 and the third at 1 p.m. They would all overlap, so that between about 1 and 2 p.m. there would be three auctioneers moving up and down the field on parallel paths some fifty yards apart. The lorry park was one side of the rings and a corrugated iron contraption advertised as a men's loo, leaned into the wind on the other side. Apparently no women were expected. At one end of the rings, a portable refreshment van wafted the smell of frying onions, and language to match, over the field.

It soon dawned on me that only a very small number of the folk present were taking any interest in the auction at all. Those few that did cluster round the auctioneer and his clerk as they moved down the first line were predominantly scrap merchants and secondhand dealers. Some farmers were among them. Many of them were engaged in the rather risky business of bidding up their own lots. I did not realize this until I had attached myself to a bunch of bidders for long enough to work out what was happening. The professionals all had their own bidding signals which were well known to the auctioneer. Some winked, some twitched, some nodded or slid their cigarette into the corner of their mouth. One, the most subtle of the lot, simply shifted a stubbly, villainous leer from one side of his face to the other. They bid against each other with full-blooded and cheerful vulgarity. However, if one of them was bidding up his own lots too frequently, the others were liable by a sudden conspiracy of silence to leave him stranded. There were one or two other amateurs like me there. The fate of one of these taught me a valuable lesson.

He had plainly set his heart on a metal field gate. There were six of them in successive lots. His first mistake was to station himself by the first gate to come up, well before the auctioneer and his attendant knot of bidders drifted up to it. It was slaughter. The auctioneer started the bidding at fifteen pounds. No response. When the auctioneer enquired about fourteen pounds, the innocent waved his paper and said 'yes'. The chap who was selling the gates joined the fun. The lot was knocked down at eighteen pounds. Fortunately, the poor fellow had walked away out of earshot before the next five identical gates went at eleven pounds a time. I decided then that, if I ever did screw up the courage to bid, I would station myself next to the auctioneer and assail his ears with a quiet whisper when he asked 'Everybody done then?' for the second time.

Everybody else there was simply having a day out. They wandered up and down the lines of items commenting on them – usually unfavourably. They formed a huge queue at the refreshment van and exchanged insults with the perspiring cooks. They clustered in small groups for gossip and the exchange of old and bawdy country jokes. I was passing one of these groups, a cluster of intent faces round a big fellow with a loud voice, in time to hear the punch line – 'and he said to her "Then I've been firing blanks the last ten years".' The audience convulsed and the punch line was repeated. The audience practically rolled on the ground laughing this time and the storyteller joined them. I didn't buy a thing that day. I saw why the collectors' items were catalogued as collectors' items. I learned a lot. I made a pig of myself with hamburgers and fried onions. I enjoyed myself immensely. I was glad that going to these auctions was one of my jobs.

I arranged with the auctioneers to be put on their mailing list for future sales. They were held three times a year, in March, July and October. The next sale was the July one and I bought a lot of materials for phase three. At that sale, it seemed to be a holiday time for most of the professionals, so the bidding was anaemic. A high proportion of the lots consisted of surplus or bankrupt stock brought down from London by hard-eyed dealers in huge lorry loads. I also bought myself a lot of tools at knockdown prices, including a builder's barrow and a large extending ladder. The quiet whispering technique seemed to work. I bumped into Tink and sought his advice on a 'pig trailer needing repair'. It had sides, a chassis and two sound wheels. It lacked a bottom altogether. That must have rotted away whilst it had stood outside for years with a load of manure in it. I bought that too. I had no luck with the search for a chaff-cutter and an oat-crusher.

We had discussed quite often in the family the best way

in which the horses and ponies really could be put to work. In the October catalogue, there appeared two items in succession. One read 'an assortment of usable horse-harness'. The other read 'a Cundy de Barker in working order'. Furthermore they were for sale in the second ring. This meant that they were intended for serious use and not for collecting.

I pointed them out to the family. 'What's a Cundy de Barker?' asked Ann. 'I think it's a sort of open carriage,' I replied. 'I can't remember whether it's got two wheels or four.' The truth was that I was not sure I had ever heard of one. But I did know that horse pistols had once been called 'Barkers' and, with the name coming so soon after the horse-harness item, I was certain I was on the right track. Something for the horses to pull might come in very useful. If the price was right, I had no doubt we ought to buy it. We would have to wait and see whether it was horse size or pony size. I got rather carried away with the whole idea. I could see myself bowling along the roads, with Neptune in the shafts, going at a spanking trot and watched in awe by the whole neighbourhood.

It was a fine day for the sale. I was an old hand now. I nodded at former opponents in the bidding ring. My mouth watered at the thought of fried onions. But that could wait. I wanted to see that open carriage. 'In working order' could not mean that it was just scarred but structurally sound. That was too good to be true.

I parked the Land-Rover and surveyed the field. I could see plenty of hay platforms and trailers, but they were all in ring three. I could not see any sign of a wheeled vehicle in ring two. I went up to the auctioneer. He was a young man with a sleek brown head like a hazelnut. I liked him. He always twinkled with good humour at the bidders in his ring. 'Excuse me, where's the Cundy de Barker?' I asked. 'The what?' he replied. 'The Cundy de Barker,' I repeated. 'What number is it?' he enquired. I showed him the catalogue. It read quite clearly – 'Lot number 1103, a Cundy de Barker in working order'. 'I think you'll find it down there,' he said, pointing down the line. There was a large pile of apple boxes obscuring my view. I would find it the other side. I thanked the young man, reflected on how very pleasantly his eyes twinkled, and set off.

On the other side of the apple boxes was a wooden peg bearing the number 1103. Beside it on the ground was a pile of rather rusty metal. I remembered what it was like when someone stole my first party balloon. I prodded lot number 1103 with my toe. Gradually it dawned on me. The young lady who had typed out that catalogue had a lot to answer for. The Cundy de Barker was a de-barker, designed for peeling chestnut fencing stakes by a gentleman named Cundy.

The rate of inflation lapped at the edge of thirty per cent a year. It receded, leaving behind a thick tide mark of bankruptcy and surplus industrial capacity. The air was filled with the decaying stench of rising unemployment. Even the fabric of the village had been touched. The school was shut down. It was small and the responsible authorities were no longer prepared to foot the bill. We were sorry to lose Miss Fitch. She really knew how to open the minds of children. The church was safe already. It had been re-prieved from the threat of closure on alternate Sundays by the arrival of a new vicar before the inflation started.

Long after the worst of the crisis, I was offered a chaff-cutter and a small oat-crusher for nothing, if I was prepared to clear them off their owner's land. I took them and stored them under the newly completed phase three lean-tos together with the 'pig trailer needing repair'. When I looked with satisfaction at those substantial lean-tos, also providing shelter for our logs, straw and turkey fattening pens, I told myself that the Cundy de Barker would have been a luxury. It would have been nice though.

# 17

# Butterfly Beef

It is alarming how quickly valuable knowledge is lost to a community, because of lack of use. The laws of natural selection decree the gradual disappearance of unused physical attributes – like tails. But that takes thousands of generations. Knowledge can be lost in two generations. People who had practical experience of running vegetable allotments and so on in the last war, and are still able to recall and use the knowledge they acquired, are now in a minority – only thirty-five years after. I wonder how many people today can sex day-old chicks, let alone separate the pullets from the cockerels six weeks later. How many people know that wood-ash is good for root crops and fruit trees? Who amongst us has ever made soap by boiling together fat and the liquor called lye, made by straining water through that same wood-ash?

As we gradually supplied more of our own requirements of meat, eggs, vegetables and milk, and did more things for ourselves generally, the more we became interested in finding out how our forebears had managed the day to day running of their lives. We learnt a lot that was new to us, but which would have been matters of everyday living in the countryside less than a hundred years ago. Some of it we found in older books. Some of it we found by working out how old bits of equipment were meant to be used. These are the really rare antiques. Practically everything that was made to be worked with was thrown out as it was overtaken by labour-saving technology. There was no room to store it so most of it was simply destroyed. Quite a lot we learnt by trial and error.

We had only taken a few steps down this road of re-capturing knowledge when we realized that the saying 'waste not want not' was more than trite words used to chide children into eating up their dinners. It reflected the approach most people had to adopt to deal with the problems of surpluses. There were no deep-freezes or canning plants. Any meat that could not be kept live 'on the hoof' had to be pickled, smoked or preserved in some other way. The nearest thing to tinning was a sealing of hot fat on potted meats and cheeses. That was a pretty risky technique in the case of meat if it was to be kept for very long.

The next thing that dawned on us was that we were simply not going to have the time to put a lot of what we were finding to use. We were taking up our spare time. Most of our days were filled by living in a fast-moving modern world. For many people whose lives we were probing into, subsistence had occupied the bulk of the day at a slow laborious pace. We decided early on that making hard cheese – different from the soft cheese variety produced by straining sour milk – would take up time we could not afford. Less time-consuming, and very worthwhile, was making bread. Ann soon loved baking loaves. She said that slapping the great wodges of kneaded dough about reminded her of babies' bottoms from her nursing days.

The point was reinforced the first time the bullock heads and the offal were returned from the slaughter house. I waited until the rest of the family was in bed. By the time I had finished the work, it was the early hours of the morning. Everything was bagged in the deep-freeze, or pickling in brine. The brains were steeping in salted water in the fridge. Without the deep-freeze and the fridge there would have been hours of work ahead still. As it was, the family wondered whether it was time well spent. Dissecting a bullock's head is a crude noisy business requiring rudimentary anatomical knowledge and a lot of brute force – mainly with a cleaver and a bone-saw. I had kept them all awake. The remains of the heads were wrapped in newspaper and taking up the greater part of one dustbin. I had considered setting those bones boiling for soup. Boiling beef bones have a penetrating and lingering smell. I had decided that would be going one stage too far.

A lot of our gleanings were useful. The mysteries of chicken-keeping soon returned to us. Our hens lay best if they are unfussed. A dry warm house is essential anyway, so is a supply of grit for shell strength. But our hens respond most to being soothed and clucked to by Ann and C-J. Those two are the more placid of us. Sue and I are usually living at a higher tempo. Laying hens and hurry simply don't go together. Mark's job of killing off birds for the table includes culling the laying flock for any members that have become passengers. Removal from the chicken house takes place at night. It causes least disturbance. With all his placidity, we balk at asking Mark to get on clucking terms with those chickens during their productive life. This is not a matter of squeamishness. We think that the callousness which is associated inevitably with the killing of animals for food is better treated as an occasional necessity than a permanent virtue.

We are all agreed that the eggs of our hens are preferable to those laid in the battery production units. It is not just a matter of the taste being different. There is more of the taste. The preferred colour of eggs is simply a matter of community culture. In this country we prize deep brown eggs, like those produced by our run of Cuckoo Marans. Friends of ours from Canada tell us that, in their country, nothing is valued so highly as an egg with a gleaming white shell.

We run cockerels with our hens. We have no evidence at all that this pandering to nature encourages laying. On the contrary we have to keep an eye on one particularly lusty cock. He tends to pick on the hens who are the slowest to get out of his way. Erotic nips on the back of the neck can all too easily turn into a savage peck. If blood is drawn, other cocks immediately have a go at pecking to produce a bit more. But we have found it useful to have fertile eggs available to put under broody birds. The pullets are run on. The cockerels are fattened up for the table in the disused rabbit hutches. Moreover we have tried our hand at crossing. We have found that Cuckoo Marans crossed with Rhode Islands are good 'doers' and excellent eating. First generation crosses are often exceptionally vigorous.

Comparison between modern gardening books and those of only fifty years ago tends to emphasize that vegetable growing by private households is now largely a by-product of the wider amateur gardening cult. We are exceptionally well served in this country with supplies of vegetable seeds, pesticides, garden sundries and advice. But I think that since the war the emphasis has shifted from 'how good it tastes' to 'how good it looks'. The advice available on how to treat soil and plants is really excellent.

Ann concentrates on those vegetables which are sufficiently vigorous to compete successfully with weeds and which will store well for the winter. Salad vegetables, like lettuce and radish, are grown amongst the herbs in a small plot near the Dirt Lock. These are near the kitchen and are likely to receive an extra bit of weeding. Tomatoes are grown in large pots against the south wall of the Dirt Lock and in a small glasshouse. Shopping excursions are fairly infrequent and growing tomatoes is a convenience and probably an uneconomical one. We get plenty of green tomato chutney. One year, Ann grew aubergines and melons in the glasshouse with the tomatoes. The aubergines produced some pusillanimous purple fruits just before the first frosts. They were useless and bitter. The melons grew into a seething, intertwined, bristly jungle. The rate of increase of that jungle was fabulous. We rescued the melons from its depths. They were more educational than edible. They do better in Israel! Ann's cucumbers have been a great success though.

The main effort goes into potatoes – both new and main crop, runner beans, onions, leeks, swedes, turnips, beetroot and, of course, the green and crimson forms of spinach, beet and winter and spring greens. Purple sprouting broccoli, 'poor man's asparagus', is a godsend during the hungry gap in March. We grow a lot of marrows. We know perfectly well their nutritional value is minute, but we like them. They are nice eaten small and young with butter in summer. We think they are nicer still stuffed with our own mince in the winter. Ann keeps them by hanging them from hooks, in frost-free places, enmeshed in the legs of discarded tights. That way she is able to keep them into January and February. They would probably keep longer, but by the end of February they are all eaten.

We have had so little success with carrots, broad beans and peas that Ann has given them up. Our carrots used to behave themselves one year in three. Peas and broad beans seem to take a lot of space and hard work for a very meagre result. Sometimes we grow parsnips and, when the sandiest part of the vegetable garden is available, we grow salsify. We find this is a delicious vegetable. Ann par-boils the long fleshy roots, peels off the dark brown skin, and fries the sliced sections lightly in butter. There is a starch in salsify which digests very low down in the human bowel. This makes it an unsociable, 'family only', vegetable. The same is true of artichokes, the tuberous, windy kind. We allow ours to infest a stretch of otherwise useless ground. It is stony and heavily populated with ground elder and various bindweeds. The artichokes compete very effectively. Globe artichokes are dotted around the flower beds. The fattest heads are cut for eating either hot with butter or cold with a French dressing. The spikier heads are left as decoration like huge purple thistles. The stems and leaves of globe artichokes are excellent eating if they are blanched by being made to grow in the darkness of a thick wrapping of news-paper. Ann is particularly proud of her leeks. We have an ample supply of strawy manure and the weeds are dealt with in the spring and winter more by a process of suffo-cation than anything else. Vast colonies of small striped worms – brandlings – take the humus deep into the soil. The leeks love it and grow fat, white and delicious.

Ann is anxious for me to find the time to build a fruit cage. We lose our strawberries and raspberries to the grey squirrels. They steal in from the edge of the woods. A neighbour of my sister-in-law was chased out of her own raspberry canes by an aggressive little squirrel. It stood up on its hind legs and swore at her first! She was so angry that she took out a shotgun licence and bought herself a twelve-bore. To the consternation of her family, she stormed into the vegetable garden with the shotgun, with-out any practice or instruction. The squirrel was there again. It sat back on its tail and squinted at her, its pouched cheeks stuffed with stolen raspberries. She pointed the shot-gun at the squirrel at two yards' range and pulled the trigger. When she picked herself up off the ground, the squirrel had gone. We have never been able to get out of her whether she missed it or vaporized it. Anyway, she got more raspberries from then on.

Until I build that fruit cage, we will continue to rely on the occasional help we get from Mark and Tippy. Tippy's pet hate is grey squirrels. She was bitten by one when she was little. Mark is a dab-hand at shooting the squirrels out of the trees from his bedroom window with an air rifle. If Tippy is in the garden and spots one in a tree, she runs to the bole, ears pricked, jumping up and down with excited yaps waiting for Mark to shoot it down for her. When he does so she is on the squirrel in a flash. One quick shake and she breaks the enemy's back. It is the same technique that terriers use with rats.

The wild birds compete with us for food too. We keep the pigeons off the greens by stretching a layer of wide-mesh nylon netting in the air above them. Unless they are driven desperate for food by snow-covered ground, pigeons will not get themselves into a situation where their line of flight for escape is impeded. For this reason they will not venture under netting. We string ours high enough for Ann to walk under, with a slight drape down the sides. It acts as a pigeon deterrent wonderfully well. We work hard at harvesting blackberries, elderberries and sloes before the birds get them from the hedges. These are mostly preserved by Ann for jam. Wild rose hips are taken for jelly. The woods give us food too. I found an excellent book, produced by the Ministry of Agriculture in the last war, on edible fungi. Wild fungi have no more nourishment than the cultivated mushrooms, but some of them have subtle flavours. My favourites are Shaggy Inkcaps. They are easy to identify but must be picked when they first appear and before they start to deliquesce into the inky black mess that mysteriously ensures the propagation of their species. Sliced and lightly fried in butter, they are very good. The family are content to take my word for it.

Apart from the short interlude with the Jerseys, we have relied on the goats for milk. Goats' milk is a necessity for some people who have an allergy to cows' milk. That is, unless they do without milk altogether. Sue has found a ready market for our surplus. The authority of the Milk Marketing Board does not extend to goats' milk and, provided one identifies its origin and is scrupulous about hygiene, there is nothing to prevent its sale.

Goats' milk can have an unpleasant rank taste. We have found that this can be minimized by keeping the milking goats on a diet of mixed rolled grain and hay. If they are tethered out, to give their digestion a tuning-up with bark and twigs, we are careful to keep them away from lush green grass. Goats will have a go at anything that looks edible. A few weeks after Snowy had eaten part of my jacket, she reached out casually and ripped some tread off the tyre of a visitor's car while she was being led past it on the way to her tethering post. However much we suppress the rankness of our goats' milk, C-J will not touch it. The smell of it turns her stomach over. We import cows' milk for C-J.

We get about eleven pints of milk a day from Fancy and Mildred when their kids are weaned. If Sue has a slackening in demand from her market, Ann turns some of it into soft cheese by letting it go sour and straining it through muslin. Mixed with chopped chives, and salt and pepper, it makes a rather sharp cheese that eats well with sweet biscuits. The girls have made yoghurt with it too. But keeping the yoghurt yeast alive involves an additional regular routine. Our supplies of yoghurt are rather sporadic.

Kid meat is delicious. The nanny kids are sold to other breeders as future milking goats. The billy kids are killed for eating at between six and eight weeks. Male goats acquire both a reproductive capability, and a taste for trying it out, at a remarkably early age. They are best taken away from their mothers and sisters before they are ten weeks old for this reason. What happens to them in the wild herds, I am not quite sure. Kid meat has a glutinous texture. Ann roasts ours in a closed pan, or in tin-foil, with a good sprinkling of rosemary on it. Served up, crisp on the outside, with new potatoes and a side salad spiced with fresh French tarragon, it makes a fine dish.

We eat a lot of our own lambs. The Jacob ewe lambs are kept for sale to other breeders or to increase our flock. If they turn out well, Sue can get a higher price for the ram lambs from other breeders than they are worth to us at table. This is the main reason they are not castrated. This is different from the practice of many commercial farmers. Jacobs produce a small carcase with a darkish meat which has a very slight similarity to venison, if it is hung for two or three days after de-freezing. Nearly all our meat goes into a deep-freeze immediately after return from the slaughter house. The joints of our Jacob lambs are meaty with only a thin fat covering. We believe this to be a result of non-castration. We prefer lean meat. So the hybrid lambs are not castrated either and are juicier eating – very high quality, lean, English lamb in fact. If we get a surplus of lambs, it may be possible to organize a swap for pork with our butcher. Not with Jacob lambs though – English housewives are very conservative. Butchers cannot risk stories going round that their meat 'looks different'.

Necessity drove us to try something else that 'looked different'. It was Jersey bullock meat. After the loss of Star, and some elementary arithmetic, it was plain that Bossy and Bumble would have to be turned into beef for our own consumption the following winter. We had been told that Jersey bull calves went for canned pet food, at a pound apiece, because they were not beef animals. Even if they could be persuaded to put on weight, they were unsaleable to butchers. Channel Island cattle have yellow fat. Conventional English housewives like their beef fat a creamy white.

Bossy and Bumble were transferred to the large field which is lorded over by Seamus. There is always plenty of grass in that field and a small spring which solves the water problem nicely. The two bullocks soon put on weight at a prodigious rate – particularly Bossy. Bumble was younger, and smaller, than Bossy. One day when I was inspecting them, Tony leaned over the gate and remarked, 'The cow's well in calf again – it's time the other one was taken off her – he's a big fellow now.' Bossy trotted up to the gate and tossed his horns. A startled Tony said, 'Good Lord, I've never seen a bullock with a barrel like that on it.' Tony had farmed cattle most of his life but it was the first time he had seen a well-grown Jersey bullock.

I was curious about the outcome of our experiment with Jersey beef. The bullocks were big. They had enormous barrels. But they had prominent hip bones too. Neither of them had been de-horned and, as they grew bigger, they became just that much too playful and cheeky for my liking. They did not worry C-J though – she whacked them on the nose if they annoyed her. I felt rather less guilty than usual when I rattled the bucket of feed nuts and led the pair of them into the trailer which would transport them to the abattoir.

Two days after slaughter, the carcases were ready for inspection in our butcher's cold-store. Row upon row of sides of prime beef hung in that store maturing slowly. Provided the temperature is a degree or two above freezing, the bacteria which cause meat to go putrid are inhibited and the enzymes, naturally present in the carcase, gradually soften the tissue and tenderize the meat. It was easy to pick out Bumble – he was the smallest carcase. I could only identifying Bossy by the yellowness of the fat. Cleft in two, he was hanging by a prime Sussex carcase. There was little to choose between the two. Our butcher was scratching his head. 'I wouldn't have believed it,' he said. His father – a lean little man in his seventies – turned away from his son and gave me a wicked wink. 'In my young day,' he said, 'we used to take a lot of butterfly beef – gets its colour from the flowers of the field – makes it prettier – don't it?'

The housewives of England do not know what they are missing. Grass-fed beef – well hung before butchering – is a lean meat with a granular texture and wonderful flavour, and the yellow fat that comes with butterfly beef is tastier – as well as prettier.

# 18

# It

If you grow your own meat, you have to get over an emotional hump. It is not a rational hump – unless you are a vegetarian. But it is a big one just the same. Angus and Ogilvy brought this home to me. When they had finished their second summer with us, we decided there was no point in running them on through another winter. They would have to live out and at best would only make a small weight gain. Sue located a small private abattoir some twenty miles away that did cattle – our usual one only did pigs and sheep. She telephoned them and made the arrangements.

The day I had been secretly dreading came. I backed our general-purpose animal trailer up to the small shelter at the top of Q's field, where Sue had shut the bullocks in on her way down to work for Tony. The rattle of feed nuts on the trailer floor brought them out of the shelter and into the trailer with no trouble at all. All the way to the abattoir I was busy repressing an uneasy feeling of guilt as I thought of the trusting pair behind me, standing side by side, swaying to keep their balance, as I drove on. The worst moment came when I opened up the trailer to unload them. Angus and Ogilvy had grown up with us. When they saw human beings, they moved towards them. The abattoir stock-handlers were used to bullocks that had spent their lives being herded away from people. Handlers and bullocks were perplexed. The handlers did not know what to do. The bullocks did not know what they were supposed to do. Angus and Ogilvy could not be driven, they could only be led. In the end they followed me through the gate into the pen where they were to wait. As I left them I did not look back. I knew I would see them gazing trustingly after me with long eyelashes over large dark eyes. I made up my mind then that, although we would raise our own beef again, we would never do it with calves we had bucket reared ourselves. The risk of the animals coming too near to trusting pets was too great. I do not have the stomach for the consequences.

After that experience, I discouraged the family from giving names to animals destined for the table. With some of them it was easy. Turkeys were a good example. The very last stage three buildings were a pair of small turkey fattening pens on the southern end of the hay-barn. They were built into small lean-tos on stilts to keep the strong wire floors about two feet above ground level. Birds run in wire, clear of their own droppings, are less prone to disease. Those pens have held four turkeys each, from August to November, every year since they went up. Ann buys the young poults from a mass producer when they have been hardened off and are fit to grow on, under cover, but in the open air. We never give those turkeys names. They have not got particularly nice natures anyway. The sight of blood drawn accidentally by a scratch on one of their number excites a frenzy of spiteful pecking by the others. Ann has often had to intervene and put a dazed and battered victim in solitary confinement until it has regrown enough feathers to cover its wounds. Ann concentrates on putting the maximum amount of weight on the turkeys, at the smallest cost, in the shortest time possible.

With other animals, more appealing than turkeys, it is not so easy. Most animals have a distinct personality and unless you deliberately shut an animal away from you, it will impress that personality on you. I have never known an animal without some personality. I can still visualize my first pet – a mouse called Whiskers, who enjoyed an insanitary existence in the right-hand sleeve of my school jacket. I am sure that Whiskers and I talked extensively to one another, and I am sure the family believes me.

The lambs that go into our freezer have never caused too much upheaval. By the time they are ready to go for slaughter, they have stopped being pretty. They have reached a rather ugly teenage stage. And, anyway, they come back already cut up into anonymous joints. But billy kids have caused us a lot of difficulty. We never name them, but that does not prevent us from stopping by the goat pens to watch them. Kids are about the most appealing young creatures I have ever come across and real time wasters. The first time we took a billy kid to be slaughtered, I told Jo and Rodney about it on the way back from the horses that evening. I mentioned we had all travelled together in the Land-Rover. 'Did you let it sit on your lap?' asked Jo sweetly. I love Jo dearly, but I could have strangled her cheerfully that evening.

C-J nearly fell into the name trap. She should have known better. Seamus and bullock minding went together and in between Angus and Ogilvy, and the two Jerseys, Bossy and Bumble, came A and B. During the year that we were eating those portions of Angus and Ogilvy we had kept for ourselves, their successors had to be growing on to maturity in the bullock field C-J had found for Seamus. In the spring of that year I went to Maidstone market. I explained our requirements to a sympathetic auctioneer. Tony had given me an introduction to him. We wanted two bullocks that would grow to about eight hundredweight each during six months feeding on grass. Furthermore, since the youngest member of the family would be looking after them, we would prefer them to have been de-horned. I do not suppose the auctioneer had ever been faced with requirements expressed like that but, with exquisite courtesy, he took me on a tour of inspection down the cattle pens. We were in luck, lots 38A and 38B near enough met our requirements. They were Hereford Friesian crosses – 38A was black and white and 38B was brown and white. I had never been to a cattle market before. The auctioneer stands on a rostrum in a white coat, well above the beasts and the ring of bidders. The quiet whispering technique I had developed from the collective farm sales was not going to be of any use. If I only secured one animal, we would be in trouble. Solitary bullocks rarely stay in a field if there are other cattle around. We needed both. I secured 38A at what seemed an attractive price. 38B cost a good deal more. At the time I assumed that their seller had pushed me up when he realized I wanted both beasts. Some time later I discovered that B really was worth more than A. Apparently the beefy characteristics are carried with the Hereford's brown colouring into the hybrid progeny. Those that carry the black colouring of the Friesian do not usually put on weight so quickly.

I firmly maintained A and B as their names. I did not want the family to become involved with them. I remembered Angus and Ogilvy. We had already made the mistake of naming Bossy and Bumble. To my consternation,

C-J insisted on calling them Jimmy and Rosco, after two tennis players she was going moon-eyed over. Fortunately, she became estranged from them when they started bullying Chance, the goat who lived in the field with Seamus. I never saw it myself, but apparently they would amuse themselves in their spare time by charging round Chance in ever decreasing circles like Red Indians besieging a wagon train. Chance was tethered, so she was reduced into retreating into the middle of the bramble thickets or jumping into the lower branches of a tree, if a small one happened to be within reach. Goats can get into trees, but usually they only do it in search of food. This is how C-J found the situation one day and she spluttered her indignation for weeks. That story had a particularly happy ending. We heard of a little boy who was heartbroken because his pet goat – also an hermaphrodite – had eaten something bad for her and died. C-J suggested the obvious solution. Seamus had stopped jumping out of that field by then and no longer needed company. We heard of the pair of them a few weeks later. The small boy and Chance already adored one another and the small boy's father once again had his lawn very efficiently mown.

At one time we were uncertain how the children would react to eating animals they had known. There was never much to worry about with Mark. Mark is a carnivore and has never hesitated to kill for our larder. Ann harnessed this side of him from the time she reared birds for the table. Mark does a tidy job for her with the chickens and turkeys. Over the years he has become an efficient and fastidious despatcher, plucker, drawer and trusser of fowl. He takes a professional pride in his work and can teach other people how to tackle it. He has shown Rodney and one of Q's sons how to wring a chicken's neck. Neck wringing needs to be done properly. If the job is bungled, the chicken squawks its outraged agony and the bungler can be put off for life. Horses and bullocks may be larger than chickens, but I, for one, prefer to handle them than feathered creatures. Mark has always had the advantage of enjoying, on the one hand, a distinct dislike for the larger animals we have kept for food, during their lifetime and, on the other hand, a clinical interest in the fowls he has dealt with. Spurred on by a healthy appetite, Mark has never paused to reflect at mealtimes. Sue has developed a more complicated approach to the matter. She divides animals into two categories, 'friends' and 'others'. 'Friends' must have names. And names chosen with imagination and care. 'Friends' are normally expected to stay with us. If a 'friend' is sold, the sale can only be to a home which has been inspected and which will be open to future inspection. 'Friends' can never be eaten. Sue settled on her own word for the death of 'friends'. The word was 'it'.

I discovered this late one evening, when I came home from work. Ann and C-J were away at the time. Fleur was standing, trembling, in a vast and spreading pool of blood, on the tiles of the porch leading to the path above the lawn. Sue was kneeling beside her with her fingers inserted deep inside the bitch's vagina. An internal cyst had ruptured a major blood vessel and it was possible only to stem the flow of blood partially. Luckily for Fleur, Sue had spotted the trail of blood and followed it. Our vet had been called by Mark who, white-faced, was pacing up and down anxiously. I arrived about ten minutes before the vet. While we were waiting, Sue was telling Fleur, 'If you don't stand still – that will be *it*.' The emphasis on the word 'it' made her meaning absolutely clear. I am sure it registered with Fleur. The vet arrived in time, located and stitched the blood vessel. Sue saved Fleur from 'it' that night. So far as Sue is concerned it is all right to eat 'others', but not to gloat over the eating. 'Others' are usually left unnamed and Sue has no special death word for them. She takes the view that if you raise animals for food it is more honest to eat them yourself than to sell them for slaughter and eat somebody else's 'others' in their place.

The reaction of Mark and Sue is consistent with their attitude to animals. Sue's inclination takes her to animals bred for showing. She likes to persuade animals to work for her. Mark's inclination takes him to animals bred for sport. He likes animals to work with him. C-J only ever wanted to look after animals. She likes good companions.

This part of her nature causes C-J problems at slaughter time. It is not just that she is the youngest member of the family. She develops a softer and more sentimental relationship with the animals than the rest of us. She has always looked for the cuddly things in life. Bullocks are not easily cuddled – once they have got past the calf stage. But the day in the year that causes C-J the most anguish, is the day after the bullocks she has had charge of have gone to the abattoir. On that day, the heads, tails and offal are returned direct to us for me to deal with. They are kept in a box on the kitchen table under a large cloth waiting for my return from the office. C-J cannot bear to look at that cloth. She accepts quite calmly the idea of death in the abstract. It is the thought of concrete evidence of the death of something she has known and touched which gets to her. That thought gets to a lot of people. Ann learned to cope with it during her training as a nurse. But even so she does not like to get too involved with sorting out the contents of the box. It was with a mixture of curiosity and fearfulness that I lifted that cloth for the first time and looked at the heads of Angus and Ogilvy. I was relieved when I knew that I could compartmentalize my mind. Angus and Ogilvy went into one compartment. The lumps of bone, meat, jelly and gristle went into another.

## 19

# Shepherd's Delight

Luck, good or bad, plays a huge role in everybody's life. Luck has been with us so far as sheep are concerned. Despite our exciting introduction, our most consistently satisfying venture has been the flock of sheep.

Once we got them under control, we found sheep fairly easy to manage. Like all livestock, they should be visited night and morning – and more often at lambing time. Provided you don't over-stock the land, they need little more than good pasture to feed on. We provide ours with a mineralized salt-lick. Sheep can suffer from metabolic diseases if they are short of some trace elements. I can never remember which trace elements, but they are all in the lick. A common bacterial disease is known as 'pulpy kidney'. The kidney ceases to function and the carcase bloats quickly after death, with the fleece peeling away from a green tinged skin. We have been pretty lucky with the health of the flock. The occasional loss with infection attacking an animal weakening a little with advancing age is inevitable.

Sue took sole charge of our sheep from the time they went into Q's field. From time to time she has to collect them up and inspect them. Any sheep showing the least sign of foot trouble is smartly upended for a closer look. Sue soon learnt how to whip a sheep over in a flash. Most lowland sheep will lie quiet once you have got them on their backs. They look like large woolly maggots, paralysed by the weight of their own tummies, and bubbling at the nose and mouth. But Jacobs are very active, like the mountain breeds, and if they are in a bad mood will glare at you, kicking and struggling and generally making an awful fuss. Very occasionally Sue finds a suspicion of foot-rot. This has to be treated immediately. Foot-rot can spread through a flock like wildfire. Sue rarely has to trim their feet. The sheep like the wooded bank at the top of the field. There is plenty of ragstone through to the surface which keeps their feet worn down.

In summer Sue has to keep an eye open for 'strike'. Blowflies lay their eggs in the thick coats, preferably where there is plenty of grease and dirt. When the maggots hatch they eat the outer layer of the animal's skin clear away in an ever-broadening patch. A careless flock owner may not notice until the animal is really sick with drooping ears and great handfuls of fleece coming away from a crawling body. The best defences against strike are early shearing, a mid-summer dip and watchfulness.

To begin with the flock consisted entirely of pedigree Jacobs. Shadow was the flock ram, though often one of his sons was kept through the winter with a view to showing and subsequently selling the following summer. The first year the flock was in Q's field, Sue brought in two ewes she had taken on as orphans and raised at the house. One was a Welsh Mountain, the other was a Clun : they were kept solely for the purpose of producing hybrid lambs for the table. The following year Sue started a small flock of Suffolk ewes. The idea was that they would be taken away to be covered by a Suffolk ram. But one of them came into season early and with the help of Shadow demonstrated that a Suffolk-Jacob cross gives a really solid lamb.

Sue was particularly interested in the idea of showing the Jacobs. She had enjoyed being with animals since she was a small girl. She has abundant self-confidence, and a real flair for the handling of animals – young animals in particular. They put their trust in her very quickly. I believe a large part of her art is her matter-of-fact but energetic bustle as she works with them. The animals do not have the time to think about naughtiness. A young animal, be it colt, heifer or ram lamb being taught to lead by Sue is always moving forward with its hocks engaged actively and its ears pricked with intelligent interest.

Shadow took a first prize in the ram class for his breed in the Kent show when he was a three-year-old. He had been eighteen months in Q's field, and was in peak condition. The judges did not mark him down for his rather kempy fleece. He had been shorn shortly before the show and the coarse fibres didn't show up. Rather surprisingly he also got away with his more serious defect. The shearing had made it all too obvious that he had a heavy freckling of small dark blotches all over his undercoat. The best of the breed have a few distinct patches on a pure creamy background. Shows allowed Shadow to give full play to his vanity. He had been trained by Sue to lead in a head collar and at the Kent show he was taken for a walk every evening to the tent where Sue took her meal with the stockmen. That year Shadow was so good-looking as to be almost pretty. He was small for his breed and his horns curled tightly into the sides of his head. I think his slightly pansy look was due partly to his legs. Jacobs have clean slender legs with fine close hairs on them instead of wool. Shadow's looked spectacular because of his matching pair of shining black knees.

Shadow's showing days were short-lived. By the year after his win he had developed a very undershot jaw – not a popular fault with the judges. But he continued to sire some lovely lambs – particularly when crossed back to his mother Sixpence.

For all his effeminate looks, Shadow has always packed a prodigious butt. One spring when he was in the paddock with a shearling son, I was nearby, splitting logs. Almost as if to show that they could do it too, the pair of them demolished a small pen made of wattle fencing just for the hell of it. Then they set about demolishing each other for good measure. They stood two feet apart and rhythmically butted each other until I could stand it no more and separated them. They brought their great bosses crashing together with a bang you could have heard a good hundred yards away and yet, although the skin at the root of their horns was broken and bleeding, they were not even dazed.

By the time the flock had grown to over a dozen breeding ewes, the shelter at the top of Q's field was too small to hold them all at inspection time, or when Sue caught them up for worming. I built a small fold alongside it and Sue promptly called it Colditz. Colditz came in useful the first time we borrowed Tony's sheep dip. While the flock had been small we had simply dunked the sheep in an old bath which was already in the field when we took it on. But when dipping became compulsory again, because of scab, that technique would not do. Sue assembled the sheep in Colditz – they always came to the rattle of a bucket of pony nuts – and I backed our animal trailer up to the entrance. Every sheep had to be dipped, except the lambs which were shortly going to slaughter. One of these lambs – a badly undersized little ewe and a disgrace to the tribe – sneaked into the trailer with the others. Tony's dipping arrangements were nicely organized. A series of hurdles made a lane down which we herded the sheep. Swinging hurdles at intervals enabled us to close off the lane behind us. Before the dip was a weighing cage which we could use if we wished. After that, one by one, it was simply a question of shoving a sheep in, pushing its head down with a crook to ensure total immersion and then, with the same crook, helping it up the ramp at the other end where it stood in a pen and drained. All went well until we came to the little ewe lamb. She did not wait to be pushed. She took a flying leap into the dip, submerged herself and swam vigorously to the ramp at the far end. Once at the top of the ramp, instead of joining the others in the draining pen, she nipped round the side of the dip and jumped in again. She loved it. Every time she jumped, a great fount of sheep dip splashed high on every side. Sue couldn't catch her and she couldn't stop her. She was dripping from head to foot, but contrived somehow to keep her temper. I was unashamedly out of control with laughter, watching Sue and the ewe lamb. They looked exactly like Ernest Shepard's drawing. in *Winnie the Pooh*, of Kanga watching Baby Roo 'practising very small jumps in the sand'. I could practically hear Sue repeating A. A. Milne's lines 'just one more jump dear, then we must go home'.

Our Jacob sheep usually come into season during October. But since the experience with the Suffolk, Sue has removed Shadow, and any of his sons who are going to be used, back to the paddock at the house in early August. Any other entire ram lambs are put in the orchard that Sue had taken on originally for Splashdown and Star – the Jerseys. Those rams have either to be sold or slaughtered before that orchard is put to use at covering time. After the rams have been wormed and generally conditioned in the paddock, Sue will split the flock. Two thirds of it is kept in the lower portion of Q's field for Shadow to cover. The rest is divided, for the young rams to deal with, between the top half of Q's field and the borrowed orchard. Each ram has a harness and colour code. When the backside of any ewe shows that she has been mounted and the ram has left dye from his harness, Sue notes the date. When all bottoms are the same colour, the dye is altered. If any ewe returns to the ram and shows another colour patch, the date of that event is noted by Sue too. After Sue is sure all our ewes are in lamb, Shadow and the others are hired out to other Jacob flock owners in the district.

The whole flock spends the winter in Q's field which is opened up completely for them. There is always plenty of grass, but if there is snow on the ground, the flock is given hay, although it can make do with barley straw and a feed block as a supplement. Sue also gives hay and whole oats or sheep nuts to the lambing ewes for about six weeks before their infants are due. It is a process known rather inelegantly as 'steaming up'. I often wonder what a National Health patient attending an ante-natal clinic would say if she was told – 'you are steaming up nicely, Mrs Jones'.

The flock lambs in the open. Jacobs lamb very easily and we have had very few lambing fatalities. We have lost a Jacob lamb which was a breach presentation. The ewe could not expel the head and the lamb drowned, as it were, before Sue arrived on the scene. We have lost one Suffolk ewe who died for no apparent reason three weeks after producing two strong lambs. Sue collects mothers and newborn lambs up each morning in the lambing season and keeps them under cover in the small shelter for a couple of days only. From the dates she noted at covering time she knows who is due to lamb next. We have not lost a lamb to foxes yet. Shadow and any other rams we have are with the flock throughout lambing. And very protective they are too.

Every now and again a lamb is rejected by its mother for no apparent reason. These orphans are brought up to the house for rearing. They start off in a large rabbit hutch next to the stove. At bottle time they are brought out. Ann stands and watches with resignation while they widdle all over the kitchen floor. As much comes out one end as goes in the other. When they are strong enough, the orphans – which are a very noisy lot – are taken up to the stable. They are kept there until they are weaned and can go back to the flock. There are usually a few of Tony's orphans around too. At feeding time Sue ropes in C-J to help. They go up to the stables with teated bottles sprouting from all over them.

The end of our sheep year comes with shearing – after lambing and before showing. We have never ever been tempted to shear our own sheep. There are plenty of shearers around us who know their stuff and will do a good job for a small price. The Wool Marketing Board has always impressed us with its efficiency. The forms for us to return showing the number of fleeces we will be selling always arrive in plenty of time. The arrangements for the collection of the fleeces are very simple and the price we get for them more than covers the cost of shearing. Jacob fleeces are not simply cream and brown. They differ from each other giving a subtle colour range from off-white, through pearly grey to a deep nigger brown. We keep back a few fleeces for Ann to spin. One fleece usually lasts her less than a month. When the rest of us are particularly irritating, Ann clears her throat rather loudly and goes off to quieten down with half an hour at the spinning wheel.

If anyone ever tells me that they want to put a bit of wasteland to use, I advise them to try sheep. If you are going to run animals on land, you have to fence it securely anyway and the extra investment in three feet of sheep netting is not all that high. In my judgement, anyone who keeps their own grass-fed horse, ought to run some sheep with it anyway. Generally speaking, the area of land required to keep one large horse or two small ponies, would easily support three breeding ewes and their progeny, in addition.

Sheep and horses go very well together. Sheep prefer different herbs from those favoured by horses. This keeps the pasture's plant population properly balanced. Furthermore they are quite happy to eat the rank dark green grass that grows round the horse droppings. Horses normally use the same general area of the field as a dunging area. They will only graze it if they are driven to it by food shortage. Sheep and horses have different intestinal parasites. So, in addition to an efficient use of land and an evenly growing healthy pasture, both breeds of animal are fitter. Horse worms living in the grass are unable to complete their life cycle inside the sheep, and vice versa.

Rodney and Jo needed little encouragement to put sheep with the horses in their field. It has done wonders for their field and made them largely independent of their butcher. It has given Rodney and Jo and their three children a lot of pleasure as well. Like us, they had to learn the hard way. They started with Kents, which are rather big sheep. I can still see Rodney tobogganing down his field, towed on his tummy by a large ewe he had rugger tackled as a means of catching up for inspection purposes, with a neighbour-conscious Jo calling down to him, 'Rodney – don't swear so !'

## 20

# Absent Friends

While I have been writing this, Ann, Mark and the girls have been reminding me about all those animals who have featured in our lives in the last few years and have not yet been mentioned. They are talking, of course, about animals Sue would classify as 'friends', not 'others'.

One of our oldest friends is Terror, a white Fantail pigeon. Sue rescued him as an ugly squashy, pink and purple squab who had fallen out of his mother's nest on the rafters of the stables where we bought Pretty Thing. I never expected her to rear him, but she did. He added to the background noises, and smells, in Sue's bedroom for some weeks. He emerged a good-looking young pigeon, eager for life and quite different from the puling infant that had been admitted as a patient, bedded down on the straw-lined bottom of a cardboard box.

Terror lives in the phase one stable building. Nylon netting keeps him off the nearby vegetable garden. He does not mind. He enjoys himself pinching food from the chickens at mealtime. Terror and Bagpipes arranged their own kind of truce. Bagpipes refrained from chasing Terror when he was on the ground at feeding time. In return Terror, who usually roosts on the fluorescent light-fitting above the feed bins, did not raise his tail if Bagpipes was underneath.

Terror is a polygamist. He was hardly installed in his home, before he started conjuring wives from the skies. They were usually white Fantails like him. But a few racing pigeons dropped in from time to time for a bit of casual sex. Once he captivated a pair of beautiful Nun doves for a whole summer. The Nuns never hatched any eggs though. We were sorry about that. They are beautiful birds and a cross between their beauty and the hardiness of the Fantail would have been interesting.

By the end of each summer we are supporting a large population of pigeons. They consist of Terror, his captured wives and their offspring. Breeding goes on in all the buildings, all summer. Any possible nesting place which the pigeons do not take is commandeered by the sparrows. We never eat the squabs. That is our one complete surrender to pure sentiment. Pigeon squab is very good and the mother never seems to miss the young when they tumble out of a nest. They simply hatch another egg. Still, Terror's offspring have not featured on our menu yet.

The first year after Terror arrived we dealt with the pigeon population in our own way. We gathered them, all but Terror and the two best-looking white hen birds, into baskets, drove them into the middle of Ashdown Forest and released them. They never came back and the next year Terror started his collection all over again. We mentioned this to some friends who also had a few Fantails. They told us not to bother. The pigeons would do the job for us. We took our friends' word and awaited events. Our friends were right. In late autumn all the local Fantail colonies desert their homes and gather together in the fields on the south side of the ridge conveniently sown for them with winter wheat. There they stay for a good six weeks. What goes on, precisely, we have never worked out. But clearly there is a large element of wife swapping in it and a bit of white slaving as well. In any event, Terror, who lives on and on, returns eventually with two or three demure little females and chats them up all through the winter until it is time to put them in the family way at the first sign of spring. Once they are pregnant, his bad habits return and he builds up another collection of loose women. They are good-looking though. Terror has the best life of any male I know. He is the original male chauvinist pigeon.

The pigeon population is kept in check to a small extent by the activities of Rowdy Roo. Rowdy Roo is a small brown Burmese cat. Her real name is Honeypot Russet. That gives a hint of her colour in a rather flattering way. Her nickname gives a better idea of her nature. She is the noisiest cat we have ever had. She is always asking for something. Even if it is only to be picked up.

We have had a succession of Burmese cats in the family – browns and blues. When we moved house we had a little brown beauty called Thaia. We were told that was Burmese for star. If it was, it was very appropriate. She was a dainty little cat and really did twinkle about the place. Unfortunately she jumped out on to the drive one evening, straight under the front wheels of the Mini. C-J was distraught. Thaia was her cat. Wisely or foolishly we went straight out again to a breeder and put a kitten in C-J's lap. She was nicknamed Rowdy Roo inside a day.

Burmese cats are very affectionate. They are also great hunters and closely related to their wild jungle cousins in Burma – quite unlike the Siamese, which are of unknown wild origin. Rowdy Roo, like Thaia before her, lives off the land from April to September on field voles and young rabbits. A pigeon squab, dabbed off a ledge with a velvet paw, is by way of a savoury. She seldom troubles the wild birds. Rowdy Roo has an excellent working relationship with the dogs. She brings her young rabbits to the front doormat and scrunches her way through the head and torso, leaving entrails, hindquarters and scut for the dogs to finish off. There is rarely anything left for us to clean up. It may be gruesome, but it is efficient.

Sheba came into our life in much the same way as C-J's pony Seamus. She is a mongrel bitch – or rather ex-bitch. She is black and white and the size and general shape of a Collie – with legs like pins, as Sue rather sniffily remarks. Somewhere there is a bit of black Labrador in her. Her mother looks like – and probably is – a pure bred Collie. Sheba was the last of an accidental litter. Farming homes had been found for the rest, but Sheba was the runt. C-J heard about her and pleaded and pleaded until we gave in. The conditions involved another dent in C-J's babysitting fund. We also insisted that the puppy was spayed. Our grounds were a happy hunting ground for every lovesick dog in the neighbourhood as it was. We saw no future in adding to the attraction.

Sheba has been a great success. But we have to watch her waistline. Since we de-sexed her, she has tended to put on weight and she likes her food. She is a terrific watch-dog and guards C-J with devotion and ferocity. This is a relief to Ann. C-J has to walk through the woods to inspect Seamus and the bullocks. In the winter she has to inspect Seamus only and, during term time, this has to be done in the dark. Every now and then the buzz goes round the mothers in the village that there is somebody lurking in the woods and exposing themselves to young girls. If anybody exposed themself to C-J whilst Sheba was with her, they would be likely to finish their life singing alto in the choir.

When Sheba is not guarding C-J, she is guarding the chickens and the turkeys. I anchored the metal casing of a large refrigerator – gleaned from the corporation tip – under an elder tree near the turkey pens as a kennel for her. She had eaten its wooden predecessor. A long chain attaches her to the tree. The metal kennel is intended for use in wet weather. She never uses it though. She prefers to sit on top of it. I think it gives her a better view of what is going on and the rain never seems to worry her.

One dog left to mention is Peggity. Peggity is a tan and white bitch hunt terrier – one of Tippy's daughters – that Sue describes as 'her best friend'. She was the smallest and most aggressive pup in Tippy's one and only litter. When she was strong enough to crawl, I used to sit her on my lap. I was usually wearing a loose 'sloppy joe' pullover with a high neck. Peggity would wriggle under the pullover up my stomach and chest. On reaching the neck, she would lick her way up my face. My nose was the target and she would grasp the end and worry it with infantile squeals and growls. At first the game was very painful, but after a while she learnt to play it with a combination of gentleness and mock ferocity.

Sue decided to keep Peggity, because she showed early signs of an unusual level of intelligence and willingness to be obedient. Hunt terriers are normally difficult to train and it is rare to see them reacting obediently to any more than the simplest commands. Peggity has progressed to the stage at which she will, on command, and when she is in the mood to concentrate, walk up behind a small animal such as a heifer, Jacob lamb or nanny kid, which is being taught by Sue to lead in a head collar. This may not sound very much but, in my limited experience, it is unusual for a terrier.

One member of the family who deserves special mention is Tigger. She is my mother and Tigger is her nickname. She is an aged, but highly durable, relic of a 'Winnie the Pooh' club formed in the late twenties when the A. A. Milne *Pooh* cult was at its height. She acquired the name because she claimed that she could 'do anything'. The exception of eating thistles and climbing trees was added whimsically by my father. It is often only with the greatest difficulty that we dissuade her from entering into the more arduous of our activities in full war-paint when she is with us at weekends. However the threat that 'She would jolly well do it, if they didn't' has often served as a wonderful spur to the children. She insists on being active and likes nothing better at those weekends than to man the kitchen while the rest of us are engaged in other activities outside.

Tigger's father was the youngest member of a large Essex country family. He was young in the days when the morality of inherited wealth of any kind was of academic interest to the vast majority of the population. There was precious little wealth about. He was apprenticed to his uncle, who was a tailor, at the age of nine and taught himself most of what he knew about reading, writing and counting. The main lesson he impressed upon his own children was 'You never know what you can do until you try it.' My grandfather lived that lesson in his own life and Tigger likes to think that some of it seeped through the years and the generations and tinged the minds of that old man's great-grandchildren as they tackled some of their more unusual tasks in recent years.

## 21

# Social Contract

Sometimes people ask us 'Where has all this got you?' We usually slide round that one by replying 'We haven't finished yet' or something like that. We do not recognize the assumption that the way we live our lives must be explainable in terms of a finite purpose. We live as we do because, in our different ways, we all enjoy it.

Of course inflation and a wish to maintain our standard of living acted as a powerful stimulus. But I think we might have done it anyway – though in a more relaxed and comfortable style. We all like life in the country. We all get satisfaction out of doing things for ourselves. None of us can resist animals. Moreover, Sue had a solid determination to work with livestock. All the ingredients were there. The prospect of rising inflation was frightening. The feeling of not being able to do much about it made many people feel frustratingly impotent. That feeling of frustration was one of the things which led to our injecting four years of increasingly intense activity into our lives. For most of the time there was a lot of fun in it. For a while when high inflation was a nasty reality there was a feeling of pressing urgency as well.

As we devoted more and more of our spare time to doing things for ourselves and buying less from other people, the quality of our life altered greatly. In the urgency stages – when virtually all leisure activities were subordinated to hard slogging – often out of doors, in bad weather and at strange hours – that quality – in terms of pleasure – deteriorated. On the other hand, it did the characters of the children no harm, and most certainly taught all of us how to laugh at ourselves and with each other. Once the hard slog had been got out of the way, the change in our lives continued, but it was no longer a deterioration. Having become accustomed to being active continually, we found it difficult to kill time by doing nothing in particular. Our idea of leisure was altering. The four of us living at home – Mark was away by then – all took up additional activities to amuse ourselves. Ann spun more of the Jacob fleeces into knitting wool on a wheel. She started to delve cautiously into lacemaking as well. Sue and C-J, both of whom now had more time for boyfriends, tried their hands at spinning. Both of them decided it was an occupation for later in life. Sue had always been intrigued by leather work and she started retrieving our sheep skins from the slaughter house and tanning them. C-J got deeper and deeper into music. I was a lot more confident about making things. I designed a double glazing system using wood and a clear rigid plastic. In reality it was a highly efficient, transparent means of excluding draughts. I did the whole house at a fraction of the cost of using one of the standard kits. A standard kit would not have worked anyway. On account of the leaning the house indulges in, we do not have a rectangular window in the place. We got out of the habit of turning on the television set to see what was on. We became more selective about the programmes we watched. We did not only go for those with a high interest content. We all like the chance to see a really good film again or a high tension cops and robbers series. Cowboys and Indians were hardly ever missed.

Ann and I became altogether more careful about the way in which we used our time. As our confidence had grown so we had taken more on. And the more our horizons had widened, the more, each in our own way, we were aware of the passing of the days, the weeks and the seasons. Ann was a good deal more placid about the passing of time than I. I found it more irksome, probably because I had so much less of the day at home. The children had their ambitions heightened and they were busy and impatient to get on and fill their days with doing things. 'Doing our own thing' is an expression which means a lot to them. Whatever else can be said about our life, it has become very active.

The economic objectives of our activities have been achieved – by and large. In order to judge whether it was paying us to produce our own food, we had to use a yardstick. For this we resorted to *Farmers' Weekly*. *Farmers' Weekly* is incredibly good value for money. For a mere twenty-five pence per week, one gets up to a hundred or more large pages of print. It contains a host of informative articles and all important current farming news. We rely on it to remind us when we have to dip the sheep and a lot of other things of that nature. It also contains current market prices. We use Smithfields' prices as a yardstick for our beef and lamb and 'Farm Gate' prices for eggs and fowl. We use current retail prices for milk – treating cows' and goats' milk as the same. We do not attempt a comparison in the case of vegetables.

To calculate our costs, we take our own labour as worth nothing. After all, we were not earning anything in our spare time beforehand. All other costs are brought in, including depreciation on fixed assets like trailers, buildings and so on. Fencing is written-off over five years. The meat and milk that goes to the owners of the land we use is calculated as a cost. Income from breeding stock sold is taken as a credit.

On this basis, the most consistently rewarding propositions have been the sheep and the turkeys. The sheep have the advantage of producing breeding stock and wool as well as meat. The turkey venture has been very successful. The birds seem to like the raised pens I designed and behave as very efficient food converters in them in the four months Ann keeps them. The hens just get by, as far as egg production is concerned, and produce a clear plus as soon as the birds culled for the pot are taken into account. The goats' milk is just competitive with our milkman, but only because Sue gets a good price for her nanny kids. We credit the milk account with the billy kids as if they were lambs. We get our beef at the same price as if we went to market and bought fatstock. The only difference is that we know our animals have lived out in the fields and have not been finished on barley. Everyone seems to agree that the flavour of our beef is very good. The cows were a dead loss as far as milk was concerned. They would have been a dead loss altogether if it had not been for the conversion of Bossy and Bumble into butterfly beef. Taking into account the loss of Star and sale proceeds on Splash and Susie, we just scraped by.

Any surplus meat we have produced has been offered to friends at our *Farmers' Weekly* yardstick prices. It shows us no loss on that basis and the offer is one way of saying 'thank you' for a good deal of tolerance and kindness. We always like some of that surplus to find its way into Q's household. It is not simply that Q's field has been of enormous importance to us. Q, and his wife Jill, added to their initial generosity by taking a continuing interest in what we were doing with the field. Our bill for fencing stakes was reduced a good deal by Jill telling us of chestnut cropping in the woods near their house. We bought two hundred at half the current retail price. Ann does some bartering with her surplus hens' eggs. Young cabbage plants and some fresh vegetables as well flow into the household that way. When the Marans are laying, a half dozen of their dark brown eggs is a cheerful sort of present for invalids and anybody else who needs a bit of bucking up.

One year we sold some hay to Julia for her donkeys. Part of the proceeds were spent on buying some of Julia's watercolour sketches in return. One of them was of a fox cub. With a few strokes of a heavily filled brush on wet paper Julia had captured completely the little animal's fluffy, sly, and rather grimy, innocence. However much Julia had worked that sketch up, she could not have improved on it.

Although we have been doing a lot for ourselves we have, in some respects, become more dependent on other people than we were before. We needed Tony from the very beginning. We bothered him as little as possible but the mere fact he was there was important. We need to put out hedge cutting and hay-making. Sometimes we need to hire manpower when Mark is not around to help. We need access to abattoirs when it comes to slaughtering time. We need the vet. We need the help of our butcher when it comes to reducing the beef to manageable joints. He has been most helpful in the way he has swapped the small profit on the meat he used to sell us, against a fee for his professional services. Most of all, we have needed other people's land. On average we have been using fourteen acres of other people's land at any one time. The owners have found the idea of meat or milk, instead of rent, an attractive one. They have been able to watch it grow. If everyone made unused land available on this sort of basis, the increase in home food production would be substantial. I include commercial farmers in this. There is no doubt that the greater use of large machinery on even larger farms is throwing up an ever increasing volume of unused corners of land on which that machinery cannot be used economically. Furthermore, if every acre of land used for grazing horses and ponies was allowed to carry an additional population of sheep, as well, it would be bad news for importers of New Zealand lambs.

We have not been aiming for 'self-sufficiency' – increased 'self-efficiency' maybe. Self-sufficiency is a matter of philosophy as well as economy. A spare-time activity can never lead to self-sufficiency in either sense. A friend, a very good friend, asked me if I was sure we were not going in for 'selfish-sufficiency'. I could see his point, but I told him I thought he was on the wrong track. We have been very lucky. We could muster the resources. I could take my holidays in odd days off from the office at short notice. We used our luck for our own immediate benefit in the first instance. But, albeit on a tiny, individual scale, we have been increasing the national wealth by extra effort. In the end, as that wealth is redistributed, it increases the possibilities of future employment. There is more than one kind of social contract.

EPILOGUE

# All Change

Some months ago, Sue came up to me sadly on a Saturday morning and asked me to go and help Bagpipes. I knew what she meant. The old bird had been looking frail for some time, wandering away from his hens and not showing much interest in them. I found him keeled over where she had put him out of the cold in an empty turkey pen. He was dying. His eye was fading and the strength in his legs had gone. When I picked him up to snap his neck there was hardly anything of him except feathers, skin and bone.

The arrival of 'it' for our old friend ushered in a time of change. A story trickled through the village that Tony was selling his farm. Nobody paid too much attention at first. True, Tony was getting on a bit, but the rumour was an old one. It had cropped up in various guises before. Some years back a part of the farm had been put up for auction and then withdrawn. And some years before that 'the park' had been stripped of its turf when Tony's shoes were pinching, so to speak. But this time there was real substance in it. Tony told us that the farm was being sold as a going concern and that the Big House was going as well. He and Diana were leaving the village and taking their beautiful Arab horses with them. A week later, he told us the sale was off. According to Tony, the would-be purchaser had formed a family company to buy the farm and then been out-voted by his co-directors. The very oddness of that tale left me uneasy. I was not the only one. Perhaps Tony and Diana were looking for more money than the farm's earning power deserved.

Soon the rumours started again. Contracts were said to have been exchanged and a date fixed for the auction of the farm livestock and the machinery as well. This time Tony told nobody who the buyers were. Even Julia did not know. The village hummed and buzzed. One theory was that the farm was to be converted into vineyards. But below the seething crust of rumour a deep uneasiness persisted.

Then the murder was out. An advertisement appeared in the local paper proclaiming that London agents were to auction the farm in no less than twenty lots. Tony had sold the farm to speculators. Rape! The village was stunned. No one could believe it. The Cricket Club enquired cautiously and hopefully about its position. The pitch was on Tony's land. The relationship between the Cricket Club and Tony was almost feudal. The Club doffed its cap when Tony passed and in return he granted it protection. Once a year he exercised his seignorial rights: a match arranged by his sons was played on a Sunday and everyone invited afterwards to be entertained by Diana in the Big House. The answer to the Cricket Club scorched round from house to house. The pitch – two acres from three hundred – had not been excluded from the sale. No tenancy at any kind of rent had been reserved for the Club beyond the year's end. Tony's last act of protection had been to ask simply that the Club be treated with consideration.

During the weeks that Tony and Diana stayed, the village held its tongue. The maintenance of outward courtesy concealed a deep and growing resentment. The Big House had hurt the village. Perhaps at some time past the boot had been on the other foot. It was plain that old wounds bled and those of us who only partly knew the past kept quiet. There were too many thorns about to prick unwary feet.

The sale of the farm stock was like a pauper's funeral. There were not many sheep and bullocks and the machinery looked suddenly old and sad and tired. The auctioneers did their best to bury the wasted corpse of Tony's farm with dignity as well as profit. But calls for bids delivered with the confidence demanded by the custom of their trade as they ran the different lots rang hollow in the air. Tony and Diana, both poker-faced, looked on as the farm's entrails – as Tink said 'Every blessed thing that could be moved, down to a bag of nails' – were converted into cash. Two days later Tony and Diana slipped quietly away.

With Tony and Diana gone, moods changed. I think that, while they were still around, many of us were reluctant to prepare the defences of the village against invasion too openly. It would have smacked of retribution and, somehow, that would have added to the sourness surrounding the affair. The day the auction particulars were published we knew what we were up against. The earlier announcement of twenty lots had puzzled us. In farming terms it made such little sense. We had realized that the Big House would be separated from the farm and the cottages as well. That would come to six or seven lots. But twenty ! How simple we had been ! Everywhere the farmland ran with private houses, a field was singled out for separate sale. Those houses would have to fight or run the risk of weekend caravans or pony parks sprouting in place of Tony's neighbouring corn.

One of those fields was next to us. To make it worse, Sue grazed Pepe in that field. The right to do so on payment of a modest sum had been an important part of her wage from Tony. Now field and wage were going. Sue was deeply hurt. Tony and Diana had been kind to Sue and Sue had been their stout champion for years. The pugnacity with which she had reacted at the slightest hint of criticism of those two had faded somewhat, but the loyalty remained. Now Sue was silent. Remarks like 'after all, we don't know all the facts' were of no help. Sue could only see one sterile fact. The farm she knew so well was being defiled. Bewildered, she blotted Tony and Diana from her mind. Her anxiety for Pepe remained.

The most revealing of the speculator's moves concerned the cricket pitch. It was the very last lot of all – number twenty. A letter to the speculator's lawyer produced the answer that if the sale 'went well' it was hoped that the Club would have the chance to buy its pitch at an advantageous price. The message was clear. The pitch was hostage for our good behaviour. The Club committee wondered how it was to know, when lot twenty was finally put up, whether their new and transient overlord was pleased or not. Should they bid or sit on their thumbs and hope?

I went to see the London auctioneers. Granted an interview with a smooth-faced man, white curls set neatly on his head, I explained that the matter of the cricket pitch was causing some excitement and that mention of a letter to the press, exposing the affair to public judgement, had been made. With a seraphic smile that nice old man informed me that his firm and their client encountered such left-wing reactions each time they broke up farms and that, to put it plainly, the Cricket Club's distress was no skin off his nose, let alone his client's. Tony had been paid a fair price, he said, 'Why not look to him?' However, his client was a reasonable and generous man. The pitch would not be offered at the auction: it would be sold privately to the Club 'afterwards' and at an 'advantageous price' – if everything had 'gone well'. I produced what I hoped was a winning smile and poured out fervent thanks for such co-operation. Beneath those thanks I pondered how, with matching courtesy, and within the law of course, we could turn the auction into a nightmare for that sleek white head – without putting the Cricket Club into the ditch. If we were to be treated to a whiff of private London enterprise, we would have to use some enterprise ourselves. Left-wing reactions!

We did not have much time. Titles were perused. Long forgotten conveyances securing water rights and other easements were hauled into the light and dusted down. The strategy was laid. The Big House and cottages would have to be abandoned to the market place. The larger blocks of land should fall safely into serious farming hands. The single fields and other smaller lots threatening the peace of the village would be defended tooth and nail. A complex web of interlocking pacts was knitted up, mostly between relative newcomers to the village, like us. Neighbour would not bid against neighbour. Bid limits were agreed. Costs would be shared and boundaries settled later. It all was based on trust. Nearby cricket clubs known to be looking round were invited to look elsewhere.

One timid soul asked for reassurance that we were not all going to land in gaol for being a 'ring'. Of course we were not a 'ring' – neither legally nor morally! The law forbidding 'rings' is aimed against professional dealers conspiring together to 'damp down' sales for personal profit. We were not professionals nor did we deal in anything. And as for conspiracy, 'damping down' and personal profit – well – the truth was that we were neighbours forced to band together, spending money we did not want to spend, to save, conserve and generally look after a piece of countryside we saw as special. People do not easily work together. Had it not been for a callous touch of arrogance in the sale particulars, I believe we would have been like our ducks and surrendered to slaughter by those London foxes without a quack of protest.

One thing we did do to damp down that sale. We prepared an 'awkward questions' list. An auctioneer is honour bound to answer questions relating reasonably to the lots before they go to auction. Largely we made our list by looking through the 'special conditions of sale'. Our questions pointed out in simple terms some snags which were set out fully, in language loved by lawyers, in the glossy auction booklet. One lot obtained its water 'by custom', not 'by right'. Some land carried an obligation to keep up a track. Was there an outstanding liability for that track? And so on.

The auction day arrived. We had a stroke of luck. At the eleventh hour the Local Council ordered the preservation of every worthwhile tree on the estate. The auctioneer announced that the separate charge for timber would not now be added to the bids securing certain lots and, reddening a little, dealt as best he could with the suggestion of 'other problems' coiled neatly in our 'awkward questions' list. One question we had given to him with the blandest smile and sharpest tongue – 'Did the auctioneer reserve the right to bid for his client once his reserve was passed?' The 'yes' to that produced a damping down indeed! My white-haired London friend, seated above us on the platform, looked sharply round the room. The fight was on and, seated in our rows, we makers of those pacts concealed our fears and waited.

First came up the housing lots. They all went for horribly high amounts. The auctioneer looked pleased. Then came the farming lots. The main block – 'the park' and farmyard buildings – went for a high, but not outrageous price. And then the lots began to stick. With few exceptions, the other blocks of farming land were not competed for. The local farmers were not prepared to help line London pockets either. Lot after lot was left unsold. The awkward questions worked and those separate fields came quietly in hand and well within our limits.

The Cricket Club had a sticky time of it. The sale had not 'gone well' but, with complete honesty, we could all deny a hand in the Council's order to preserve the trees. After all, we were in an area of outstanding natural beauty. The attempt to take an extra sum for standing timber had invited intervention. As for the thinness of the bidding and those questions, we all did our best to sound innocent, without telling lies. The other side was not deceived. The Cricket Club was made to wait until most of the unsold lots had gone to private buyers and then had to argue its head off to get a chink of advantage in the price. But it got the pitch. The lack of other buyers must have helped.

Things are settling down again now and in a little while the episode will be forgotten. The next ordnance survey will record the new boundary lines and officially seal the past. Soon there will be new people in the Big House. But the binding link between the village and the house has gone forever. With the farm split up, it is now simply a large, lovely, lonely house of no great social or economic moment. Those bidding pacts, and the knowledge of them, have welded the village together in a subtly different form, quite separate from the house. The new joined up to protect the old and, in doing so, became part of the old itself.

Changes – exciting changes – are on the way for us at home. Together with neighbouring friends we bought the field that Pepe grazes in. We will have the use of our friends' portion in exchange for the annual delivery of fat lambs for their freezer. We are making plans for our new land – six acres – the biggest piece of land we have ever owned ourselves. Just along the cart track from our house, it commands the finest view for miles and, complete with copse and spring, swoops down in dips and hollows towards more fields below.

The chance to buy that field could not have come at a happier time – part of that auction wind blew good for us. Sue has finished a year at agricultural college and has just started on a spell in London, learning saddlery. For the moment, she lives with us at home. An early start and a late finish sees the animals cared for. But, engaged to marry, Sue is planning new homes for her goats and sheep, two nice young horses, and a Jersey cow as well, near where her home will be. Sue has never lacked determination and her knack of finding sheds and fields still stands her in good stead. Pepe will be sold to a nice home to see out his working days. He needs more comfort than Sue can really manage. C-J has plans to bring Seamus nearer home. She thinks she might try a cow as well. She saw a Dexter calf at the South of England show and has been broody ever since. Ann wants her own sheep, a mixed flock, to give her different wools to spin. With turkeys, chicks and vegetables at home, Q's field is just a little too far away – our new field next door will do just fine. If Q still lets us use his field, it will go for hay and I might take the bullocks on myself – or join forces with another family. That auction taught a lot about co-operation. All the rescued fields will be put to productive use.

With all the goings on, some things have got a little out of hand. Peggity is in disgrace. Upstairs in the whelping box in Sue's bedroom are five unplanned puppies. There is one chance in three that they are proper hunt terriers. Sue is not worried. She says she can rely on her 'best friend's' good taste. I am not so sure. By the colour of those pups I would say Peggity is night blind. Sheba is laughing over the whole affair. That is one side of life she doesn't have to worry over. Tippy is waiting for Mark to come home and take her rabbiting in the new field. Fleur is snoozing her life away in noisy slobbery bliss. She is always lying in the sun or with Rowdy Roo by the boiler. We still lock her in at night. Those dustbins are not all that far away.

The Frog must be restocked. We left the guinea-fowl's wings unclipped too long. One day last summer they flew. The last we saw of them they were disappearing, alternately whirring and gliding like huge grey partridges as they winged down towards the weald. Quackers, the duck who escaped from the foxes is there. So is the old Cuckoo Maran who got the stiff neck. Snapdragon, the little pale grey hen we bred, keeps them company. She has not laid a small egg for pickling for a long time. Last autumn the old Maran went broody. Ann popped some eggs under her and one blackberry chick hatched out. Every evening, from the day it was born, the little chicken hopped on to the old hen's back to be flown by her mother into the branches of the holly tree. There they roosted until daybreak – safe from foxes. New guinea-fowl would not suit those old age pensioners – too noisy. We might get more bantams though.

The garden must be regained. Four years of extremes of weather and lack of my attention has let loose a natural evolution. Some plants have thrived and kept the weeds at bay. Others have silently succumbed to the strangle of creeping grasses. In some places the garden and the wild have intermarried. We have huge patches of dwarf willow-herb ablush with myriads of autumn cyclamen. Those patches must be cherished and planned round. More change.

The other night I looked up at the ridge. How many changes have you seen? I thought. The trees sighed down to me. The trees are the spirits of the ridge. The trees and the ridge will never change – and the ridge will be here forever.

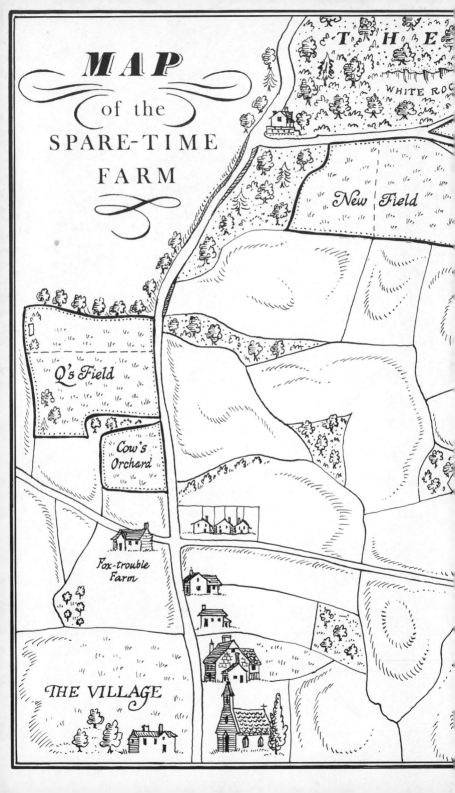